D0126655

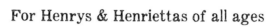

For Henrys & Henriettas of all ages

CONTENTS

TIME LINE

1817 July 12, David Henry Thoreau born in Concord, Massachusetts

1822 Thoreau first visits Walden Pond with his family

1837 August 30, Thoreau graduates from Harvard College

October 22, Thoreau starts writing in a journal, prompted by Ralph Waldo Emerson

1839–1841 Henry and brother John teach at Concord Academy

1839 August–September, Henry and brother John paddle the Concord and Merrimack Rivers

1840–1844 The *Dial* is published; Thoreau contributes seven essays and four poems

1842 January 11, John Thoreau Jr., Henry's brother, dies

July 19–22, Thoreau and Richard Fuller walk to Mount Wachusett

1843 May–December, Thoreau lives on Staten Island, New York

1844 July–August, Thoreau walks across western New England

1845 March, the Fitchburg Railroad line is completed

July 4, Thoreau moves into his house at Walden Pond

1846 July, Thoreau spends a night in jail for not paying a tax

August–September, Thoreau makes his first trip to the Maine woods

1847 September 6, Thoreau leaves his Walden Pond house

1848 January–February, Thoreau reads "Relation of Individual to the State" in Concord

1849 May, "Resistance to Civil Government" is published in *Aesthetic Papers*

May 26, *A Week on the Concord and Merrimack Rivers* is published

1849   June 14, Helen Thoreau, Henry's older sister, dies

October, Thoreau and Ellery Channing make their first trip to Cape Cod

1850   June, Thoreau travels to Cape Cod

September, Fugitive Slave Law passes

September, Thoreau and Ellery Channing travel to present-day Quebec

1852   September 6–7, Thoreau and Ellery Channing hike Mount Monadnock

1853   September, Thoreau makes his second trip to the Maine woods

1854   May 30, the Kansas-Nebraska Act becomes law

July 4, Thoreau reads "Slavery in Massachusetts" lecture in Framingham

August 9, *Walden; or, Life in the Woods* is published

October 19–21, Thoreau revisits Mount Wachusett

1855   July, Thoreau and Ellery Channing travel to Cape Cod

1856   September 5–10, Thoreau takes botanical trip to Brattleboro, Vermont

1857   June, Thoreau makes his last trip to Cape Cod

July–August, Thoreau makes his last trip to the Maine woods

1858   June 2–4, Thoreau and H. G. O. Blake hike Mount Monadnock

July 2–19, Thoreau and Edward Hoar travel to White Mountains

1859   February 3, John Thoreau, Henry's father, dies

October 16, John Brown attacks the armory at Harpers Ferry, Virginia

October–November, Henry reads "A Plea for Captain John Brown" in Concord, Boston, and Worcester

December 2, John Brown is hanged

1860   August 4–9, Thoreau and Ellery Channing hike Mount Monadnock

1861   April 12, the American Civil War begins with firing upon Fort Sumter

May–July, Thoreau and Horace Mann Jr. travel to Minnesota

1862   May 6, Henry Thoreau dies at home in Concord

1863–1866   *Excursions, The Maine Woods, Cape Cod,* and *A Yankee in Canada* are published posthumously

WHAT MAKES HENRY THOREAU IMPORTANT?

> I should not talk so much about myself
> if there were anybody else whom I knew as well.
> —*Walden*

Henry Thoreau is most remembered for living for two years at Walden Pond in Concord, Massachusetts, and for spending one night in jail for refusing to pay a state tax. He lived only to the age of 44 and did not become famous in his lifetime. Yet more than a century and a half after his death, we still read his essays and books. We still print his words on posters and greeting cards. Why?

The first answer is a simple one. We can relate to what Henry saw and experienced in the mid-1800s. Our times may be different but the ways that people think, act, and react are very much the same. Our concerns about laws and government may be similar to his. Our connections with nature can be as close and as personal for us as they were for him. Henry's words reach out to us from across time and point out the realities that lie right in front of our noses. His insights sound so true that it's almost as if he were here to read our minds or to give us advice in person. How did this man become a symbol for American independence and for environmentalism? You'll learn more about Henry here.

Today's rebuilt North Bridge.

Rob DePaolo

1

AT HOME IN CONCORD

David Henry Thoreau was born on July 12, 1817, in Concord, Massachusetts. His parents, John Thoreau and Cynthia (Dunbar) Thoreau, already had two small children: five-year-old Helen and two-year-old John Jr. John was a quiet man. Cynthia was an outspoken woman. The family lived in part of a farmhouse that Cynthia had grown up in as a teen.

Henry's father was trying to make a living as both a storekeeper and a farmer. Unfortunately, his timing was bad—1816 was known to many as the "Year Without a Summer." On the other side of the planet, an Indonesian volcano named Tambora had erupted in 1815. It sent so much thick ash into the Earth's atmosphere that it affected the next growing season in North America and northern Europe. People living in Massachusetts saw frost in every month of 1816. More northern states and Canada had snow in every month. As a result, many crops didn't have a chance to grow well, or even at all. Anyone who raised vegetables for others had problems producing enough to sell.

Although conditions were better the following year, the Thoreaus decided to leave the farm and move closer to the town center. They left Concord altogether in 1818. They spent several years in Chelmsford and in Boston. John Thoreau worked at various jobs, most often as a store manager. By March 1823, the Thoreaus came back

The center of Concord in 1839, from John Warner Barber's *Historical Collections*, 1841. *From the author's collection*

to Concord for good. They brought with them a new member of the family, baby Sophia (so-FYE-ah), who was two years younger than Henry.

A Revolutionary Town

Concord was the oldest inland town in the nation and was founded in 1635. Native Americans and later white English colonists settled where the Assabet and Sudbury Rivers met to form the Concord River. The town sat 20 miles west of the Massachusetts state capital of Boston. Concord was known as a country town or an agricultural town. It had a courthouse and was a seat of government for Middlesex County. But it was also famous for its history. Here, shots were exchanged between colonial minutemen and British soldiers on April 19, 1775. The gunfire that took place at the North Bridge marked the beginning of the American Revolutionary War.

Here people passed Revolutionary era sites every day. The road they took to Lexington was the same route the redcoats had used when they marched from Boston. Back then, some of the soldiers had gathered at Wright's Tavern, right in the center of Concord. The minister's house still sat within sight of the battleground. But the wooden bridge itself had been gone for many years. The gray stone walls on both riverbanks marked where it once stood.

To young Henry, the town had more to offer than just the Main Street businesses, homes, and history. There was a whole natural world

Pronouncing "Thoreau"

As you talk with people about Henry Thoreau, you will hear them pronounce his last name in two different ways. Some will say "thih-ROW," with the accent on the last syllable. Some will say, "THOR-oh," with the accent on the first syllable, sounding almost like the word "thorough." How did Henry and his family pronounce it?

Clues can be found in Henry's own writings. Once he made fun of his name and claimed that his ancestors worshipped Thor, the god of thunder and lightning in Norse mythology. He used forms of the word "thorough" at times to describe himself, too. He seemed to favor the accent on the first syllable.

Notes from friends who heard his name firsthand agree. Bronson Alcott, Nathaniel Hawthorne, Daniel Ricketson, and Edward Emerson referred to him in their writings as "Thorow," "Thoro," or even "Thorough." They spelled his name the way it sounded to them.

Today people use both versions. But the one like "thorough" is probably the correct one.

to explore. "I think I could write a poem to be called 'Concord,'" he said later. "For argument I should have the River, the Woods, the Ponds, the Hills, the Fields, the Swamps and Meadows, the Streets and Buildings, and the Villagers. Then Morning, Noon, and Evening, Spring, Summer, Autumn, and Winter, Night, Indian Summer, and the Mountains in the Horizon." Henry and his brother John spent their days outside whenever they were free from school. All of Concord was their playground.

A Boyhood on the Pond

One of the most interesting spots within Concord's borders was Walden Pond, a lake that was about a mile south of Main Street. Henry was only five years old when he first saw it. He always remembered how he felt at this new sight. He and his family had come from Boston to visit his grandmother, and they made a special trip to the pond. "That woodland vision for a long time made the drapery of my dreams," Henry said. To his child's eyes, it was beautiful and peaceful. It was not at all like busy Boston, which then had more than 43,000 residents. Here at Walden, it was as if "sunshine and shadow were the only inhabitants" among the pine trees. It would be a great place to live someday, he thought.

Henry was thin and had brown hair and gray-green eyes. But when people first met him, they focused on his large nose. Some said it looked like an eagle's beak, or like the one they'd seen

The New England Town

In the six states that make up the New England region, the word "town" means something different than it does in other parts of the country or the world. Here, a town is a larger defined area and a unit of government, not just a close community of homes and businesses. Other parts of the United States would call this a township or even a county.

In the early days, life in each town centered around one church that stood near a common, an empty yard intended to be shared by everyone. This small settlement was surrounded by mostly open land at first. As more people arrived, they bought property and built houses farther away from the church and the common. But they were still residents of the town.

Henry once wrote, "I have travelled a good deal in Concord." He meant that he did more than just wander the streets where people lived. He explored the fields, hills, swamps, rivers, ponds, and woods within its borders, too. The Town of Concord covered 25 square miles, or 16,520 acres of land. Henry was familiar with every part of it. He didn't have to go "out of town" to find something interesting.

on a bust of Caesar, the ancient Roman emperor. Henry was just as quiet and serious as a judge, they said. "Judge" even became one of his nicknames. The truth was that he felt comfortable being alone, without a lot of others chattering around him. "I would rather sit on a pumpkin and have it all to myself than be crowded on a velvet cushion," he said. And exploring the fields and woods around town restored his energy and gave him time to think. He loved to walk or to

Explore Your Town's History

Henry loved Concord. He wrote this note in his journal on December 5, 1856: "I have never gotten over my surprise that I should have been born into the most estimable place in all the world, and in the very nick of time, too."

Your hometown may not be as famous as his, and it may not attract as many tourists. But yours has an important story behind it. What is it?

WHAT YOU NEED

- A print or online town history, if one exists
- The archive of a local historical society, if one exists
- Conversations with older residents

Using these resources, try to learn the answers to these questions:

- When was the town founded?
- How was it named?
- Why did people come to live here at first?
- Why do they live here now?
- Where is the oldest building?
- Are any historic sites open to the public? (If so, visit them.)
- Are any sites listed on the National Register of Historic Places? (If so, visit them.)
- What main businesses have been here through the years?
- Did any important events ever happen here?
- Do you hold any annual events or celebrations?
- Is anyone "famous" from here, from the past or from the present? If so, where did they live?

What can you do with the details you learn?

- You can become an informal tour guide to friends and out-of-town visitors.
- You can create a walking tour of important sites.
- You can create a brochure that promotes your town's best and most important features.
- You can begin to write a history of your town, if none exists.
- You can even organize a town historical society, if none exists.

Learn more about your place, and be proud of it!

"saunter" by himself, or with a friend he could trust.

The Thoreaus had returned to Concord in 1823 to join the family business of making pencils. Cynthia Thoreau's brother, Charles Dunbar, had discovered a graphite supply in New Hampshire. He and business partner Cyrus Stow used it to make Dunbar & Stow pencils. When Stow left the partnership, Charles invited John Thoreau to take his place. They changed the name to John Thoreau & Company. At the time, the best pencils were imported from Germany and France. American pencils were often made of gritty lead and were difficult to write with. They smudged the paper. Thoreau pencils were of higher quality, and they began to sell well.

After John Jr. and Henry graduated from the Concord Academy, the family decided it could only afford to send one brother to Harvard College. They chose Henry. At the end of August 1833, he and his friend Charles Stearns Wheeler traveled the fifteen miles to Cambridge, to their shared room in Hollis Hall. Except for some time away due to illness and to teach elsewhere for a few months, Henry spent the next four years there.

An Independent Learner

Harvard College was founded in Cambridge in 1636, just one year after the town of Concord. By 1833, it was still the only college located in eastern Massachusetts. Many men in New England came

(*left*) Young Henry Thoreau, based on the Samuel Worcester Rowse crayon portrait in the Concord Free Public Library.
The Thoreau Institute at Walden Woods

(*right*) A Thoreau pencil box label.
The Thoreau Society and The Thoreau Institute at Walden Woods

ONE GROSS
SUPERIOR GRADUATED
DRAWING PENCILS,
—FOR—
ARTISTS, ENGINEERS, &c.
1, 2, 3, 4,
MANUFACTURED BY
JOHN THOREAU & CO.
CONCORD, MASS.

to Harvard to get a good education. Henry was lucky enough to live within walking distance of it.

He took the standard courses in English, history, mathematics, natural and intellectual philosophy, Greek, and Latin. The professors' lectures weren't all that inspirational, however. Students were rarely asked to participate actively in class. And if Henry wanted to walk to the banks of the Charles River to study nature in person, he had to do it on his own. Field trips were unheard of.

For him, the best part of Harvard was its library. There he could read and learn about anything he wanted to. He taught himself the basics of French, German, Italian, and Spanish. He read books of English poetry. He began a habit of copying favorite passages into special notebooks so he could review them later. Even after he graduated on August 30, 1837—ranked as number 19 in a class of 50—he continued to check out books from the college library as an alumnus. He did this for the rest of his life.

A Harvard man could choose from among four possible careers: doctor, lawyer, minister, or teacher. But people could also teach without earning college degrees. Henry's older siblings, Helen and John, both taught in Taunton, about 50 miles southeast of Concord.

In the fall of 1837, Henry got a job with the Concord public schools. He was one of two teachers assigned to the first floor of a brick building in the town center. The building was otherwise used for meetings by the adult men's group the Masons. During the weekdays, about 50 students crowded into each classroom. Both were cramped and noisy.

Henry had been teaching for almost two weeks when he was visited by a member of the school committee. (In other parts of the country, this group may be called the school board.) The man was shocked at how unruly the students were. He told Henry to discipline the children immediately. Henry didn't think a nonteacher—and an elected official, at that—should be giving a real teacher such advice. He picked out several students at random and smacked the tops of their hands with a ferule, a ruler-like piece of wood used for punishment. Those who were chosen were upset. They had known their teacher as a kind person. It was unlike him to be violent without reason. Later that day, Henry resigned from the job. No one was going to tell him what to do.

Soon Henry did something else that was unusual. He changed his name. His official given name was David Henry Thoreau, even though his family members always called him Henry. Now he switched the names around and began signing his name as Henry David Thoreau. He didn't ask any town or government agency to make the change official. He just started using it this way.

A Well-Respected Friend

People in Concord thought Henry was odd. First, he left a decent teaching job at a time when

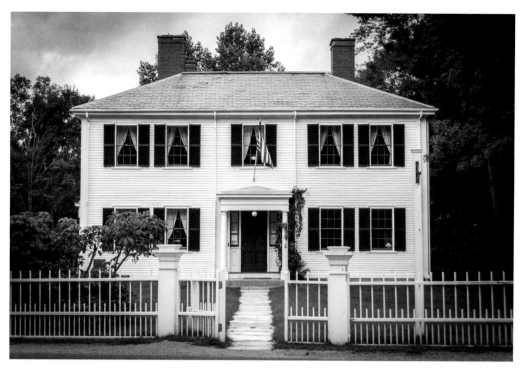

money and jobs were tough to come by. And then he changed his name! Henry was certainly not a typical young man.

He had at least one well-respected friend in town. Ralph Waldo Emerson was a noteworthy writer and lecturer who lived in a large white house on the road to Cambridge. Although he was born in Boston, he had close ties to Concord. His grandfather, William Emerson, had been the first minister to live in the parish house near the North Bridge.

Waldo, as his friends called him, was a Harvard graduate who had served as a minister in Boston. He resigned when he realized he no longer believed in some of the rituals of the church.

In 1834, he boarded with his step-grandfather and current minister Ezra Ripley at his house by the North Bridge. Here he wrote his beliefs in his first book, called *Nature*. As part of Henry's graduation day at Harvard, Emerson spoke on "The American Scholar." He encouraged Americans to think for themselves, to develop their own culture, and to leave European traditions behind.

On the Fourth of July, 1837, Concord celebrated the country's independence by dedicating a granite tower monument at the North Bridge site. To honor the event, a choir sang a four-stanza poem written by Emerson. Henry was among the singers. The poem began:

(*left*) Ralph Waldo Emerson in an 1881 lithography by Gerarde A. Klucken.
National Portrait Gallery, Smithsonian Institution/Art Resource, NY

(*right*) The Emerson House today.
Rob DePaolo

What Is Transcendentalism?

Henry and his best friends were transcendentalists. This did not mean they were part of a club, an organized movement, or a religion. If transcendentalists were in the same place at the same time, it was because they wanted to meet and talk with "like-minded men and women," said Frederic Henry Hedge. Otherwise, they were independent writers and philosophers who loved nature and trusted their instincts. They thought they could each find God and a spiritual connection to the universe by spending time outside and in the natural world, and not by sitting in a church pew, listening to a minister preach or read verses. Transcendentalism was a way of looking at religion that went against what a lot of people believed at the time. Its "members" were often viewed as radicals.

Transcendentalism began in America when Ralph Waldo Emerson published his first book, *Nature*, in 1836. "The happiest man is he who learns from nature the lesson of worship," he wrote. His words influenced other writers who felt the same way. Because Emerson lived in Concord, that was where transcendentalism was based in the mid-1800s. Henry was one of Emerson's followers and friends. Other transcendentalists included Bronson Alcott, Ellery Channing, Margaret Fuller, Frederic Henry Hedge, Theodore Parker, George Ripley, and Jones Very.

Emerson had not invented transcendental ideas. They could be traced to Europe and to the works of German philosophers and writers like Johann Gottlieb Fichte, Johann Wolfgang von Goethe, and Immanuel Kant. Transcendentalism could also be found in the essays and poetry of British writers Thomas Carlyle, Samuel Taylor Coleridge, and William Wordsworth. The Americans read and were inspired by the writings of these men, as well as those by their own acknowledged leader, Ralph Waldo Emerson.

By the rude bridge that arched the flood,
Their flag to April's breeze unfurled,
Here once the embattled farmers stood
And fired the shot heard round the world.

Emerson started a second American revolution by beginning the transcendentalist movement in Concord. He became a mentor to Henry and to other writers and philosophers, who often gathered at his home for conversations. Henry even lived there on occasion, helping take care of the Emerson family.

A New Lifelong Habit

Keeping a journal or writing in a daily diary was something that many people did in the 1800s, especially the transcendentalists. Sometimes they would loan their journals to friends so they could read each others' opinions and discuss them together later.

On October 22, 1837, Waldo Emerson asked Henry if he kept a journal. His young friend started one immediately. Henry wrote entries nearly every day for the rest of his life, filling 33 notebooks. Sometimes he took parts of these writings and created longer essays, lectures, or even books from them. Henry also contributed seven essays and four poems to the *Dial*, the transcendentalist magazine that was published in the early 1840s.

Keep a Daily Journal

"In a journal it is important in a few words to describe the weather, or character of the day, as it affects our feelings. That which was so important at the time cannot be unimportant to remember." Henry wrote this advice in his own journal on February 5, 1855. He often began his entries with notes about the weather. Then he wrote observations about nature and people, and included what he thought on a variety of subjects. Sometimes he drew small pictures. Sometimes he took ideas from his journal and put them into his essays and books.

You can keep your own private journal and write whatever you wish, as often as you wish.

WHAT YOU NEED

- ❧ Notebook or journal with blank pages
- ❧ Pen or pencil
- ❧ Computer with word processing (optional)

What will you write? The choice is yours. You can write about:

➡ what you see

➡ what you smell

➡ what you hear

➡ what you feel

➡ what you think

➡ what you believe

You can write stories or poems. You can draw. You can add pictures and mementos, like a scrapbook. Write as much or as little as the day suggests.

You can write in the evening and record what happened during the day. You can take your journal outside and describe what you see in nature. You can use it during some of the other activities featured in this book. You can use it long after you have finished this book. Some people keep journals or diaries for their entire lives.

Some of Henry's journal books.
The Pierpoint Morgan Library/Art Resource, NY

Brothers and Friends

Henry helped with the Thoreau pencil business. He set out to improve the consistency of the lead. Something needed to be added to the graphite to make handwriting flow easier. Henry experimented with wax, glue, whale oil, and with different mixtures of each of them. When he instead added local clay to the graphite, the quality of Thoreau pencils grew better than ever.

Henry and his brother John set out on a two-week adventure at the end of August 1839. They paddled down the Concord River, merged into the Merrimack River, and headed north into New Hampshire. They passed the many bustling brick mill buildings of Lowell, Massachusetts, and Manchester, New Hampshire, in a boat they had made themselves. It was 15-feet long, 3½ feet wide at the middle, and was "painted green below, with a border of blue, with reference to the two elements in which it was to spend its existence," Henry said, meaning the grassy riverbanks and the blue sky. They called it *Musketaquid*, which was the Native American name for Concord. It meant "grassy plain" or "grass-ground river."

After six days on the water, they stowed their boat and continued on foot and by stagecoach to the White Mountains. They saw the stony profile of the Old Man of the Mountain and made it all the way to the top of Mount Washington, the highest peak in the Northeast. After a few days of hiking and camping, they took a stage back to their boat. They traveled faster with the Merrimack current and got back home on September 13. It had been quite a trip.

By now, the brothers were spending a lot of time together. They ran their own school. Henry had organized a home-based class in the fall of 1838. By the spring of 1839, he attracted more students than he could handle. John joined him as a teacher, and they moved their classes to another building in town. Here boys and girls could study composition, grammar, geography, geometry, algebra, natural philosophy (science), Greek, and Latin. They drew maps of the country, outlining all 26 states and some of the western territories. And the Thoreaus took the children on afternoon field trips, too. Everyone could see firsthand the plants and animals that lived in their neighborhoods. They found the best places to pick huckleberries and blackberries. They learned how to plant gardens and how to fix boats. Sometimes they even sailed out on the rivers or ponds.

The Thoreau brothers had very different personalities. John was more outgoing and was the kind of man who could joke, play, and turn somersaults with the children on the school lawn. Henry was more thoughtful and somewhat standoffish, but was "not disagreeable," said one. Both men could relate to the students in their own ways. Paired together, they taught lessons not only from books, but also from real life. And they used no ferules or physical punishments in their classrooms, just expectations that the work was to be done. This arrangement seemed like the best possible one for a good education.

Conduct a Plant Inventory

"About half a dozen years ago I found myself again attending to plants with more method, looking out the name of each one and remembering it. . . . I wanted to know my neighbors, if possible, —to get a little nearer to them." Henry wrote this note in his journal on December 4, 1856. You can get to know what plants are in your neighborhood, too. You may be surprised at how many are here.

WHAT YOU NEED

- A piece of land that you care about and have access to: a backyard, a school property, a park, or a playground (and one that is not treated with chemicals)
- Plant identification books from your local library or science teacher
- A 72-inch-long piece of yarn, string, or rope
- Journal, paper, or computer spreadsheet
- Pen or pencil
- Camera (optional)

This activity may be best done in summer or early fall, when flowers and leaves have grown. What you find depends upon your habitat and the season.

Decide how much of the land you are going to inventory. Look around and start with the biggest plants first: trees, then bushes or shrubs. List each one on a line in your journal. (You could type them into a computer spreadsheet later.) If you don't know a name, just describe it in words. For example: "Shrub with small round leaves, gets red berries in fall." You can add a drawing, too. Move to the taller flowers and plants, like ferns or flowers. Add each one to the list.

Save the lawn for last. Tie the ends of the string together to make a circle. Place the circle on the lawn. It will serve as a sample for the whole yard. How many plants can you find within the circle that are not thin blades of grass? How many different kinds of grasses are here? Write them down.

When your list is done, look at the plant guidebooks to find the common and scientific names. Having a detailed inventory will help you keep a phenology later, if you wish. This is a larger project where you keep track of when flowers blossom, when leaves appear, and when trees change color. See "Keep a Phenology" in chapter 6.

11

The parish house, which Nathaniel Hawthorne called "the Old Manse."
Rob DePaolo

Unfortunately, the Thoreaus had to close their two-room school after only two years. John's health was not good, and he felt weak. He got terrible nosebleeds. He also showed signs of consumption, today known as tuberculosis. This contagious lung disease affected a large number of people in that time. The only recommended cure was to breathe fresh air, and doing this didn't really solve the problem. Henry had a mild bout of consumption while he was at Harvard. Waldo Emerson's first wife, Ellen, had died of it.

On January 1, 1842, John was sharpening his razor when he accidentally cut his finger. He pressed the cut back together and bandaged it. Some days later, he saw that the wound had become infected. John had gotten tetanus, or lockjaw. Back then, this was not a curable disease. He began to suffer from intense pain, muscle spasms, and stiffness in his jaw, making it difficult to swallow. Family members and friends watched his condition worsen day after day, and they and the doctors could do nothing to help. When he died on January 11 in Henry's arms, John was only 27 years old.

Henry had lost not only his brother but also his best friend. Being the sensitive person that he was, it is perhaps not a surprise that he began to show the same symptoms of lockjaw. He had not been cut, and he had no real infection. These were just sympathetic pains. But they were very real to him and to anyone who saw him. Everyone was afraid Henry was going to die, too. Gradually and slowly, his health returned. For many years, he still got teary-eyed whenever he thought of John or heard his name mentioned.

Tragedy found the Emerson house, too. Little five-year-old Waldo Emerson got sick at the end of January. He died several days later of scarlet fever. His father and Henry shared their grief at their mutual and unexpected losses. It was a lot for both men to bear.

A View of the River

By summer, Henry felt well enough again to spend more hours outside. He planted a garden at the minister's house next to the Concord River as a wedding present for short-story writer Nathaniel Hawthorne and his wife, Sophia. The newlyweds began renting the home in July. They would be able to use the vegetables and herbs later in the season.

Henry also took Nathaniel out in his boat for a paddle along the river. Nathaniel was amazed by how slowly the water moved. "I had lived three weeks beside it before it grew quite clear to my perception which way the current flowed," he said. A month later, he bought the boat from Henry so he could try paddling it himself. He was only sorry he could not also "acquire the aquatic skill of the original owner." Nathaniel was impressed by a flower that grew in the water. "The fragrant white pond-lily abounds, generally selecting a position just so far from the river's brink that it cannot be grasped save at the hazard of plunging in," he said. He decided to change the name of his new boat from *Musketaquid* to *Pond-Lily*.

Henry kept busy. He helped his father manage the pencil business. He read travel narratives. He wrote journal entries, poetry, and essays. And he spent a lot of time walking through the woods and fields, studying nature, and paying attention to what the plants and animals did and when they did it. He thought about things that other people never noticed: like how animals and humans can accidentally pick up seeds from plants and spread them to other places. Children eventually started bringing him dead animals to identify.

One September day, Henry got a humorous idea after seeing a problem his sister had. "Grasshoppers have been very abundant in dry fields for two or three weeks. Sophia walked through the Depot Field a fortnight ago, and when she got home picked fifty or sixty from her skirts, —for she wore hoops and crinoline. Would not this be a good way to clear a field of them, —to send a bevy of fashionably dressed ladies across a field and leave them to clean their skirts when they get home?" He probably laughed out loud at this amusing solution to insect management.

A New York Adventure

In spring 1843, Waldo Emerson got Henry a teaching job in New York. Waldo's brother William Emerson served as a county judge on Staten Island. He needed someone to tutor his oldest son, seven-year-old Willie. Henry moved south and spent eight months living with the family, teaching the boy (and his younger brothers, Haven and Charles), and exploring the natural habitat of the island and the nearby bays of the Hudson River. He took the ferry across the river and met several influential individuals in New York City.

But even with the better opportunities for writing and publishing that this place could offer, it would never feel like home to Henry. He went back to Concord to visit his family for Thanksgiving, and was reluctant to return to the island and the Emersons afterward.

Women like Sophia Thoreau wore crinoline dresses with hoop skirts.
From the author's collection

Record Wild Animal Behavior

"I spend a considerable portion of my time observing the habits of wild animals, my brute neighbors. By their various movements and migrations they fetch the year about to me." —Journal, March 23, 1856

In each season, Henry watched wild animals and wrote about what he saw. He was fascinated by their behaviors. You can make similar observations and record what you see. Remember, the word "wild" does not automatically mean "scary" or "hurtful." In this case, it refers to an animal that isn't tame and that lives in its natural environment.

ADULT SUPERVISION REQUIRED

WHAT YOU NEED

- Paper and pen or pencil
- Sit-upon (something dry and comfortable to sit upon)
- Binoculars (optional)
- Camera (optional)

Find a natural place that doesn't have much interference from people. It can be an old field, a forest, a beach, or a grassland. It can be a trail at a park, a nature preserve, or a wildlife refuge. It can even be your own backyard, if you can get away from domestic animals (cats, dogs, farm animals) and visitors to feeders (birds, squirrels). These creatures are either too used to humans or too much like us to be considered wild.

Sit down and make yourself comfortable. Turn off any electronic device that could make a sound. Be quiet and don't talk, even if another person is with you. Try not to move much. It will take about 10 to 15 minutes for the animals in the area to decide that you are harmless and to appear. While you are waiting, you could listen deliberately and draw a sound map (see chapter 2).

Be alert for any kind of movement and for any kind of animal. It can be big or small. It can be an ant, a butterfly, a bird, a chipmunk, a turtle, a snake, or a deer. Or it can be something else altogether. Part of the fun here is not knowing ahead of time what will show up.

When you finally see an animal, watch it closely. Watch it for as long as you can see it. The first animal may leave and another one may show up. Stay in one place for at least 30 minutes. If you have them, use a pair of binoculars to get a better look. Keep your pen and paper ready, but spend most of your time watching. What does the animal look like? What do you think it is doing? Is it looking for food? Is it eating? Is it collecting material for a nest? Is it alone, or does it have others with it? Do not talk to the animal or move toward it. Let it act as naturally as possible.

Write down a few words that describe the animal. What are its colors? How does it move? What sounds does it make? You can even try drawing the animal, but spend most of your time watching it. You may want to take its photograph too, but be careful. The click or the flash of the camera may disturb the animal and draw its attention to you. As a result, it may change its behavior or even leave or hide. Watch first. Take a picture later, if you wish.

When the animal has left—or when you think you have watched it long enough—go back home. Look at your notes and drawings, and write a longer description that records exactly what you saw and where. Write as though you want to explain it to someone who wasn't able to see it in person. Can you imitate the animal's motions? Can you act them out for others?

Learn more about the animal, including its scientific name. Compare your description with what others have seen and learned. Check wildlife guidebooks at your library, and look online to see what photos others have posted and what encounters they have had. Your state government's website should include pages for departments dealing with conservation,

environmental protection, or natural resources. Often these will provide lists of species found in your area, as well as photos and descriptions of the animals themselves. Cornell University's All About Birds site (www.allaboutbirds.org) is an additional terrific resource for identifying birds.

You may want to return to the place where you first saw the animal a week, a month, or a season later. Is it still there? Does it look the same? Is it acting the same way? Write and draw what you see again. Add your new notes to your previous ones.

Henry could reach into a box of pencils and bring out exactly a dozen in one hand.

The Thoreau Institute at Walden Woods

By the end of December, he was back home for good. He never taught formally or for pay again. And although he traveled regularly around New England, he never moved away from his hometown again, either.

Your Pencils Today

He was back to work with the pencil business, trying to figure out ways to improve production and sales. Thanks to Henry's efforts, Thoreau pencils soon became available in a range of four graphite thicknesses: S (soft), H (hard), S.S. (softer than soft), and H.H. (harder than hard). These variations could also be shown as numbers from one to four, with one being S.S. and four being H.H. Today the most popular pencil we use is labeled as a number two. We can thank Henry for this.

Thoreau pencils continued to win awards for high quality at regional exhibitions in 1847 and 1849. By 1853, other companies had improved their pencils enough that the competition became too challenging. The Thoreaus found a better market by selling the graphite as a raw material instead. They ran their business this way until Henry himself passed away in 1862. When someone asked him why he didn't continue to improve the pencils, Henry replied, "Why should I? I would not do again what I have done once."

Concord Conflagration

At the end of April 1844, Henry and his friend Edward Hoar took a rowboat out on the Sudbury River. They expected to spend a few days exploring and camping along its banks. They were still within the Concord town boundaries when they caught some fish and decided to cook them for an early lunch. They landed at Fair Haven Bay, where they built a fire on a tree stump. Both of them should have known better. "The earth was uncommonly dry," Henry later admitted. Their small campfire soon spread to the nearby grasses and began to burn its way up the hillside. The men stomped on the flames to try to stop them, but too much loose tinder was lying around, and the fire was too quick for only the two of them to handle.

"Well, where will this end?" Edward asked.

Both men already knew the answer. "It will go to town," Henry confirmed aloud. They couldn't let this happen. They needed to warn people and get help fast.

Edward hopped into the boat to paddle back. Henry ran through the woods as smoke filtered through the trees behind him. He found the owner of a nearby property and another farmer, and they returned to the fire. Soon the alarm bell rang in town. Other Concordians were now on their way with buckets, hoes, and shovels. Henry sat on the hilltop to catch his breath and to watch, at first. Then he joined his townspeople in fighting the fire. It took them several hours to get it under control and finally put it out. Curious, Henry later walked back through the then-blackened woods. He found the fish well broiled and lying on the burned grass.

A few days later, the story appeared in the *Concord Freeman*. More than 300 acres had been burned, it said. At least three landowners' properties had sustained a total of $2,000 in damages. Henry and Edward were not named in the article. But everyone knew who was responsible.

The fire, we understand, was communicated to the woods through the thoughtlessness of two of our citizens, who kindled it in a pine stump, near the Pond, for the purpose of making a chowder. As every thing around them was as combustible almost as a fireship, the flames spread with rapidity, and hours elapsed before it could be subdued. It is to be hoped that this unfortunate result of sheer carelessness, will be borne in mind by those who may visit the woods in future for recreation.

Woodlots were valuable. People needed wood supplies to build houses, to cook meals, and to stay warm. The fact that Henry committed this accidental arson with Edward Hoar was probably what saved both men from facing criminal charges. Edward's father was Samuel "Squire" Hoar, a former legislator and the most respected man in Concord. He may have paid the property owners to cover part of their losses.

At first, Henry felt "like a guilty person, — nothing but shame and regret." But the more he thought about it, the more he believed that the farmers should have been paying closer attention to their woodlots all along. Never mind that the Fitchburg Railroad locomotive often sent hot coals flying into the same woods, burning them regularly along its tracks. No one ever complained whenever the railroad company damaged a property.

Still, after the fire, a number of townspeople shook their heads at Henry. They called him a "damned rascal." They looked at him with anger and disapproval whenever they thought of the "burnt woods." Honestly! What would Henry Thoreau do next?

Transcendentalist Ellery Channing moved to Concord in April 1843 and soon became one of Henry's good friends.

The Thoreau Institute at Walden Woods

The replica of the house at Walden Pond.

Rob DePaolo

2

WALDEN POND, A WEEK, AND *WALDEN*

Three and a half years had passed since John Thoreau died. Henry still missed his brother and longtime best friend. He decided to write a book about the boat trip they had taken to New Hampshire in 1839. Writing it would be a way to honor John and remember their good times together.

A Quiet Place to Write

By now, Thoreau wrote in his journal regularly. He contributed a few pieces to the *Dial*, the transcendentalist magazine. One of his travel essays was published in a Boston magazine. But a book was a much bigger project. To get it done, he thought he should get away from home. The Thoreau household must have been a hectic place at times. It could be full of boarders, maiden aunts, and the antislavery activists that his mother and sisters were involved with. Henry needed time and a space to himself. What could he do?

An answer came from his friend Ellery Channing, who was then working for the *Tribune* in New York, and who understood what Thoreau was after. Channing sensed from a previous letter he had gotten that his Concord friend was miserable and frustrated. He wrote back on March 5, 1845: "I see nothing for you in this earth but that field which I once christened 'Briars'; go out upon that, build yourself a hut, & there begin the grand process of devouring yourself alive. I (*right*) Henry's brother, John Thoreau Jr. (1815–1842). The painting is titled *Portrait of a Man*, attributed to Naham Ball Onthank of Boston, Massachusetts.

Concord Museum, www.concordmuseum.org

(*above*) Henry's drawings of two boaters reflected in the water, from his journal, August 16, 1854.

The Thoreau Institute at Walden Woods

see no alternative, no other hope for you." Known as a solitary and unreliable wanderer himself, Channing was convinced that Thoreau would benefit from living on his own. He just had to take the risk and go for it.

Channing's answer was the right push for Thoreau. Ralph Waldo Emerson had bought fourteen acres of woodland along the north shore of Walden Pond some months earlier. Thoreau asked for permission to live here, and Emerson gave it. Thoreau chose a spot that overlooked a large cove, and he began to make plans. He had just helped his family build a new house on Texas Street, not far from the Concord railroad station. Putting up a smaller one-room building wouldn't be as difficult. He borrowed an ax from Bronson Alcott and began cutting down trees to form timbers and rafters. He dug a cellar into the hillside and laid a foundation for a chimney. His new home was taking shape.

Now that the nearby Fitchburg Railroad line was finished, the Irish rail workers were leaving the area. James Collins was one of them. He sold Henry his wooden shanty for about eight dollars. Henry used its boards as fresh lumber. On a pleasant day at the beginning of May, a team of eight friends—Emerson, Alcott, George William Curtis, Sherman Tuttle, and Edmund Hosmer and his three sons, John, Edmund, and Andrew—helped Thoreau raise the framework. The shanty boards were nailed onto its outer walls, and the roof was finished. In the end, the house measured 10 feet by 15 feet. It had a peaked roof, a root cellar, a window on each side wall, and a door facing the pond. The materials had cost him $28.12½. Today the same supplies would run between $700 and $900, without considering the price of labor.

The Fitchburg Railroad

When railroads began to be built across New England in the early 1840s, businessman Alvah Crocker (1801–1874) saw potential. He owned a paper mill beside the Nashua River in Fitchburg, a town in north central Massachusetts. A railroad could solve his problem of quickly and safely getting his products to market in Boston, 50 miles away.

Of course, the trains would be able to carry passengers, too. But for Crocker and the other mill owners working in the inland towns, the main goal of the tracks was to haul goods from their small factories into cities such as Boston.

Crocker was the leader of the project. He sailed to England to buy iron for the rails. He stopped at the docks in Boston harbor and convinced immigrants arriving from Ireland to work for him. They were hired to do the physical labor: grading the soil, installing the wooden ties, placing the iron rails upon them, and hammering home the heavy spikes. The Irish families built temporary homes of wood—shanties—along the route and moved down the line as they finished each section.

In 1843, the workers started building the railroad at its eastern end in Charlestown, just across the Charles River from Boston. When they reached the 20-mile mark of Concord in early June 1844—running right along the western edge of Walden Pond—an announcement in the *Boston Post* promoted the trip:

The scenery is romantic and pleasing, and a ride to old Concord by railroad cars will be found very different thing from that of stage coaching the same distance. It is expected to make the run in one hour from Boston, including the time required to cross from State street to Charlestown depot—and three to four hours are now generally consumed to accomplishing the same by the stage.

The tracks finally reached Fitchburg in early March 1845. Now it would take only two and a half hours to make the complete 50-mile trip. Later the eastern end of the line was finished; it ran to Boston and into a large castle-like station, complete with an assembly hall.

By the time Thoreau moved to his Walden house, trains could pass by the pond up to eight times a day. Locomotives spit black smoke and cinders as they pulled their cars east toward Boston or west toward Fitchburg.

At first he complained about the smoke and the noise. But he, like many other Concordians and New Englanders, used the train frequently to travel from one town to another. And he could appreciate the role the railroads began to play in American commerce. Concord wasn't quite as rural anymore. He wrote:

I am refreshed and expanded when the freight train rattles past me, and I smell the stores which go dispensing their odors all the way from Long Wharf [Boston] to Lake Champlain [Vermont], reminding me of foreign parts, of coral reefs, and Indian oceans, and tropical climes, and the extent of the globe. I feel more like a citizen of the world.

Alvah Crocker built more railroad lines heading farther west, past Fitchburg and north into Vermont. During the second half of the 1800s, trains stopped at Walden Pond and dropped off visitors to its amusement park.

Today the Fitchburg commuter line is part of the Massachusetts Bay Transit Authority (MBTA). More than two dozen trains pass Walden Pond each weekday, and more than a dozen do on typical Saturdays and Sundays. The ride from Concord to Boston takes about 40 to 45 minutes.

The House on Walden Pond

On July 4, 1845—eight days before his 28th birthday—Henry Thoreau moved into his one-room Walden home. Inside, he had a desk to write on and a small bed for sleeping. "I had three chairs in my house," he said. "One for solitude, two for friendship, three for society." And a whole world of nature waited just outside his doorstep, ready for exploration. His time was his own. Here he could live as simply as he wanted to.

Sketch based on drawing by D. J. Strain, from Frank Torrey Robinson's *Living New England Artists*, S. E. Cassino, 1888.

From the author's collection

He wrote: "I went to the woods because I wished to live deliberately, to front only the essential facts of life, and see if I could not learn what it had to teach, and not, when I came to die, discover that I had not lived. . . . I wanted to live deep and suck out all the marrow of life. . . . It is worth the while to have lived a primitive wilderness life at some time, to know what are, after all, the necessaries of life and what methods society has taken to supply them." He made a practice of beginning his days by bathing in the pond.

Here Thoreau could study nature in each season. He could watch the fish, birds, and small mammals that lived in and around the pond. He could go exploring and collect samples of flowers and other plants. These he tucked into his "botany-box hat," which had a shelf inside, perched above his hair. This way, his hands and arms were free for taking notes or for moving branches aside as he walked. "I think that I cannot preserve my health and spirits, unless I spend four hours a day at least—and it is commonly more than that—sauntering through the woods and over the hills and fields, absolutely free from worldly engagements." What a wonderful opportunity he had! "To be awake is to be alive," he wrote. Too many people were not paying attention to the natural world around them. Henry felt sorry for them.

He was also able to study Walden and the neighboring ponds: Flints' Pond, Goose Pond, and White Pond. He liked to paddle his boat to the middle of Walden, then lie back on the seats. He watched the clouds pass above him as if in a

Build Your Own Walden House

"I have thus a tight shingled and plastered house, ten feet wide by fifteen long, and eight-feet posts, with a garret and a closet, a large window on each side, two trap-doors, one door at the end, and a brick fireplace opposite." This is how Henry described his house at Walden.

You can use your imagination or even use real materials to build a house similar to the one he lived in for two years.

WHAT YOU NEED

- Masking tape
- Tape measure

OPTIONAL SUPPLIES

- Rope
- Blankets or sheets
- Large empty cardboard boxes
- Scissors
- Packing tape

In a large empty space, like a basement, a backyard, a park, or a driveway, use the masking tape and tape measure to mark a rectangle on the ground, ten feet by fifteen feet. Remove a section of the tape in the middle of one end to represent a front door. Add a box just inside the opposite end to mark the fireplace.

Step inside the large box, your "house." Can you believe that Thoreau had a single-sized bed, a small desk, three chairs, and a woodstove in here? Where would you put each one, if you had them? If you have real extra furniture that you can borrow, place them inside the house.

If you outline your house near trees, you may be able to tie a rope around the trunks about four feet above the ground. Then drape old blankets or sheets over the rope to make walls for the house.

Or, if you have large pieces of cardboard left over from packing boxes, you can cut walls to size. Tape the edges together and arrange them around the rectangle. You may have to bend the bottom edges a bit for the cardboard to stand straight.

Your Walden house can be a temporary one that you have for just one day, or for any day you want to create it. Or you can set it up as a more permanent structure in a place that's not in the way of everyday life or business.

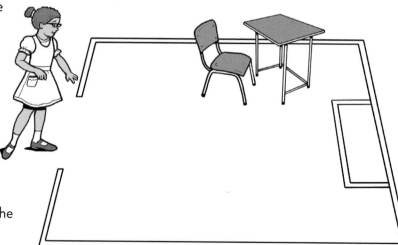

dream, "until I was aroused by the boat touching the sand, and arose to see what shore my fates had impelled me to."

Thoreau also cleared two and a half acres of Emerson's land to create his own vegetable garden. He planted beans, peas, potatoes, and turnips. Such a large plot required a lot of attention, however. "I was determined to know beans," he said. "When they were growing, I used to hoe from five o'clock in the morning till noon, and commonly spent the rest of the day about other affairs. . . . He who eats the fruit, should at least plant the seed," he said. Some of the food he ate. Most of it he sold. Henry kept track of how much he spent on seeds and equipment and how much he made in sales. He decided to abandon the planting during his second year at the pond. It had not been a profitable enough task for him.

Solitude was something that Henry enjoyed at Walden Pond. But he was not completely alone all of the time. A dirt road led right past his house and his bean field, and people passed by on their way to Lincoln or Sudbury. Alcott, Emerson, and Channing visited him on occasion.

Other folks from Concord were curious about Henry's behavior. They thought it was odd. First he changed his name. Then he left a good teaching job in town and created his own school. Now he was living by himself in the woods. Why?

Henry was not a hermit. He didn't stay at Walden every minute of every day. His house sat only a mile away from the center of Concord. He could walk back along the railroad tracks

and could visit or have dinner with his family or the Emersons. He could run errands to the Main Street businesses. He could take his laundry along so that his mother or the household servants could wash it for him (as any young 19th-century man would have done, in his place). He even left Concord entirely for several weeks when the chance came to take a trip to Mount Katahdin, in the Maine woods. But Henry always returned to his comfortable house at the pond.

He was busy thinking about and writing his book, too. It was turning out to be much more than a travel narrative. He described what he and John had seen and done as they had paddled north along the Concord and Merrimack Rivers, then hiked into the White Mountains and to Mount Washington. But he added stories of his other hikes to Mount Wachusett and Mount Greylock, too. He put many of his philosophical views into the chapters. He talked about boating, nature, religion, writing, friendship, and even love. He included original poems. He also used some creative magic to cut the trip's thirteen days down to seven so readers would be able to better follow the story.

"All Nature Is My Bride"

Remembering John and their adventure probably brought back memories of someone else. At the time of their trip, Henry and John were in love with the same woman. Her name was Ellen Sewall and she was from Scituate, a coastal town south of Boston. Six weeks earlier, she had

Henry's sketch of a skunk, from his journal, March 10, 1854.
The Thoreau Institute at Walden Woods

Draw a Sound Map

"Sometimes, in a summer morning, having taken my accustomed bath, I sat in my sunny doorway from sunrise till noon, rapt in a revery, amidst the pines and hickories and sumachs, in undisturbed solitude and stillness, while the birds sang around or flitted noiseless through the house, until by the sun falling in at my west window, or the noise of some travellers' wagon on the distant highway, I was reminded of the lapse of time."

Imagine sitting still for hours at a time, just listening to the world around you! Henry did this at Walden Pond. You can practice listening, too—and draw what you hear on your own sound map.

WHAT YOU NEED

- Paper, notebook, or journal
- Pen or pencil
- A natural place to sit or stand
- Watch or timer

Find a place outside to sit or stand comfortably. Hold your notebook lengthwise so that the wider part runs from left to right. Draw yourself as a small figure in the middle of the page.

Be as still as you can, and listen. When you hear a sound, make a mark on the page in the direction that you heard it. If it came from your left, draw on the left side of the page. If you know what made the sound, you can write its name, like "bird," "leaves rustle in wind," "truck," and so on. If you don't know the source, then use lines or designs to imitate the sound.

Listen for as many minutes as years you have been alive. If you are twelve years old, then listen for at least twelve minutes. You may stay longer, if you wish.

When you are done, look at your finished sound map. How full is it? What was your favorite sound? What was your least favorite? Did you hear any curious noises that you want to investigate?

You can do this activity anywhere and at any time—on your own or with other people. At the end of a group session, share your results with the others.

Different people will notice different sounds.

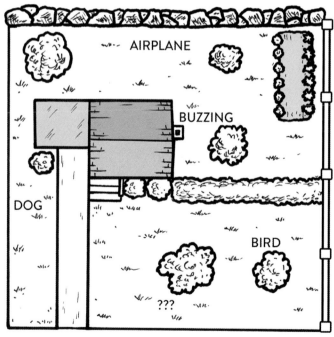

Plant and Tend a Garden

"Making the earth say beans instead of grass—this was my daily work." Henry also planted peas, potatoes, and turnips in his two-acre garden during the first year he lived at Walden Pond.

Planting and maintaining a garden can be as simple as putting seeds in soil and waiting for them to grow. Or, you can create a garden large enough to help feed your family throughout the year. Your only limits are imagination, available space, and some time for watering, weeding, and harvesting.

ADULT SUPERVISION REQUIRED

WHAT YOU NEED

- Indoors: Small metal or plastic containers, awl, scissors, potting soil, scoop, seeds, water

- Outdoors: Shovel, seeds, mulch, water, information about your habitat and growing season

For an indoor garden:
Raid your recycling bin for empty containers that are several inches deep. Soup cans and yogurt cups are good examples. You could cut off the tops of larger plastic jugs, too. Use an awl or another sharp tool to punch a few holes around the bottom edges for drainage. Find a shallow container that you can rest the others in, to

capture moisture. Fill each can or cup with potting soil. Push a seed into each one, not more than an inch deep. Sprinkle water over each seed. Find a sunny spot to keep the pots. Water them whenever the soil feels dry. Your garden should begin to grow within a week or two. Be patient! It will be a while before you can harvest your crops.

For an outdoor garden:
Remove the grass and weeds from a plot of land that measures at least three feet square. Use a shovel to loosen all of the soil and create two rows for planting. Check with local gardeners or reference books for the best times to plant the kinds of seeds you have. Once you have pushed your seeds into the rows, be sure to add mulch (chopped-up bark or lawn clippings) around

them. Water your garden whenever the soil is dry, or when no rain has fallen in several days.

What will you grow?
Indoors, you can grow cooking herbs like basil, mint, parsley, sage, and thyme. You can also grow beans, peas, peppers, and radishes. If you have room, and plenty of sunlight, try growing tomatoes.

The same plants will work for outdoor gardens during normal growing seasons. You can also add carrots, cucumbers, potatoes, strawberries, and even pumpkins and squash, if you have a lot of room.

Where will you get the seeds? See the "Collect and Swap Seeds" activity in chapter 5 for ideas.

Henry's surveying compass and tripod.
Concord Free Public Library

arrived in Concord to visit friends. Both Thoreaus met Ellen and liked her immediately. They each went on walks with her. Henry began to write poems and journal entries about her. Even though she was in Concord for just two weeks, Ellen had impressed the brothers. She seemed to like them, too. But she had gone back home. She must have been on both of their minds as they paddled their boat north and hiked in the mountains. As soon as the Thoreaus returned from their river trip, John hurried off to Scituate to visit Ellen.

During the next year, both men visited and corresponded with Ellen. Each one eventually, separately, proposed marriage. Ellen accepted John's proposal at first, but she had to quickly break off the engagement. Her father was a conservative man who did not want his daughter to be tied to any transcendentalists. She turned down Henry, too.

By the time Henry was writing about the boat trip, Ellen Sewall had been married to Unitarian minister Joseph Osgood for more than a year. In spite of their emotional history, Henry kept in touch with Ellen and her husband. A few years later, he stopped to visit their home in Cohasset on his way to Cape Cod. He even gave them one of his handmade wooden boxes for collecting geological specimens.

Henry never found such romance again. Instead, he focused his energies on his outdoor explorations, his studies of nature, and his writing. He wrote, "How rarely a man's love for

nature becomes a ruling principle with him, like a youth's affection for a maiden, but more enduring! All nature is my bride." He found enough projects on his own to keep himself occupied.

A New Profession

One of those projects was to teach himself the science of surveying land. He and John had introduced the basic method to their Concord Academy students years earlier. Now Henry set out to survey a sixty-one-acre body of water instead: Walden Pond. He waited until winter came, when a thick layer of ice covered the water. He drilled more than a hundred sounding holes in it. He carefully measured distances from one hole to the other, and from one shore to the other. The task took him a great deal of time and attention. When he was done, he had the most accurate map of Walden Pond ever drawn. And he learned much by creating and completing it.

Henry would later buy professional equipment and advertise his services to the public as a land surveyor. For the rest of his life, this job was one that paid him the most and was perhaps the most rewarding. He surveyed properties for the town of Concord and for private landowners there and in neighboring towns. The act of surveying gave him the chance to work outside, earn a bit of money, and do a bit of natural exploration at the same time. Surveyors had to be detail oriented and precise in their measurements. Henry was already used to doing this, as he kept track of the dates when local plants emerged and bloomed. He was used to using tools to learn more about the natural landscape. "What wonderful discoveries have been, and may still be, made, with a plumb-line, a level, a surveyor's compass, a thermometer, and a barometer!" he said.

Leaving Walden

Henry decided to leave his Walden house at the beginning of September 1847. Waldo Emerson had plans to travel to Europe, and his wife, Lidian, and their children would be left behind. Waldo asked Henry to move into the Emerson home and be the temporary man of the house. After his stay of two years, two months, and two days at the pond, he felt that it was time to leave, anyway. "I left the woods for as good a reason as I went there," he said. "Perhaps it seemed to me that I had several more lives to live, and could not spare any more time for that one."

His choice to retreat to Walden had been worthwhile. "I learned this, at least, by my experiment: that if one advances confidently in the direction of his dreams, and endeavors to live the life which he has imagined, he will meet with a success unexpected in common hours." When he left his one-room house for the last time, Henry had a decent draft of his travel book, as well as one about his woodland experience.

Henry paid to print one thousand copies of *A Week on the Concord and Merrimack Rivers* in 1849.

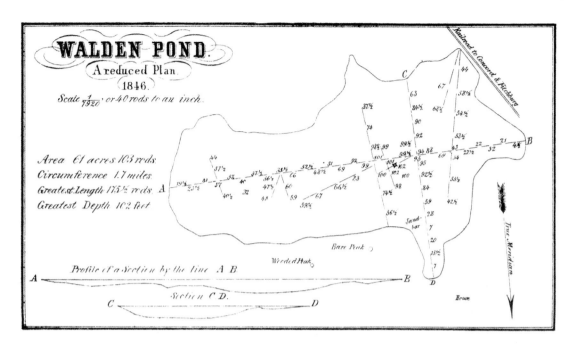

The book got average reviews and didn't sell well. In the next four years, only 219 copies were sold, and 75 others were given away. The publisher shipped the remaining 706 books back to Henry. Box by box, he hauled them up two flights of stairs to his attic bedroom in the Thoreau family home. "I have now a library of nearly nine hundred volumes, over seven hundred of which I wrote myself," he wrote, seeing the humor in the situation.

His first book was not a success. It hadn't made him rich or famous. But Henry wasn't going to stop writing. "Nevertheless, in spite of this result, sitting beside the inert mass of my works, I take up my pen to-night to record what thought or experience I may have had, with as much satisfaction as ever. Indeed, I believe

Henry's survey of Walden Pond.
The Thoreau Institute at Walden Woods

Walk Off a Quarter-Acre Lot

"I have lately been surveying the Walden woods so extensively and minutely that I now see it mapped in my mind's eye—as, indeed, on paper—as so many men's wood-lots, and am aware when I walk there that I am at any given moment passing from such a one's wood-lot to another's."

Henry was an experienced and respected land surveyor. He could walk across a property and estimate its general size without using his tools. You can learn how to do this without having any special equipment.

ADULT SUPERVISION REQUIRED

WHAT YOU NEED

- A large outdoor space (preferably flat), like a playground or an empty parking lot
- Masking tape
- Tape measure

First, measure the length of your average step. Find a sidewalk or a large empty floor space. Mark a line with a short piece of masking tape. Put both of your feet behind the line. Then walk normally across the space for five steps. Mark a line at your last step, at the tips of your toes, with more tape. Measure how many inches you have walked, from one line to the other. Divide the number by five. The result is your average step length in inches.

Once you know your step length, you can walk anywhere in a straight line, count your steps, and estimate how far you have come.

Now you need to know some surveying terms:

An **acre** is a unit of land measurement. An acre is often rectangular in shape, but it can vary widely. The area inside the rectangle has to be equal to 4,840 square yards or 160 square rods. To find the area of such a piece of land, you must multiply its length by its width.

A **rod** is a unit of length that equals 16.5 feet or 5.5 yards. Rods measure the edges of an acre.

A **quarter-acre lot** (¼ of an acre) could measure 4 rods by 10 rods (66 feet by 165 feet, or 792 inches by 1,980 inches).

At your large open area, see if you can walk along the sides of a rectangle this big.

How many steps will you need for each side? Divide both 792 inches and 1,980 inches by your step length to find out how many to take. Then count your steps out loud as you walk. You may need a friend to walk with you to keep track of the numbers. Later, use the tape measure to see how close you came to the correct length.

If your area doesn't match this rectangle, try a quarter-acre lot with another outline:

2 rods by 20 rods (33 feet by 330 feet, or 396 inches by 3,960 inches)

5 rods by 8 rods (82.5 feet by 132 feet, or 990 inches by 1,584 inches)

6 rods by 6.67 rods (99 feet by 110 feet, or 1,188 inches by 1,320 inches)

Can you measure other properties now?

Measure the Depth of Water

"It is remarkable how long men will believe in the bottomlessness of a pond without taking the trouble to sound it. . . . I can assure my readers that Walden has a reasonably tight bottom at a not unreasonable, though at an unusual, depth. I fathomed it easily with a cod-line and a stone weighing about a pound and a half, and could tell accurately when the stone left the bottom, by having to pull so much harder before the water got underneath to help me. The greatest depth was exactly one hundred and two feet." In this instance, Henry uses the words sound and fathom to mean "to measure the depth of a body of water."

Can you re-enact how Henry measured the deepest part of Walden Pond?

ADULT SUPERVISION REQUIRED

WHAT YOU NEED

- ❧ A body of water: a pond, a lake, or even a swimming pool
- ❧ A long rope or string
- ❧ A stone, or something heavy but portable
- ❧ A ruler or yardstick
- ❧ A marker
- ❧ A boat or raft (optional)

Practice first with a bathtub or a kitchen sink, using a thinner string and a smaller weight. Tie the weight to the end of the string. Fill the tub or sink with water. Hold one end of the string and drop the weight

into the water. Let it land on the bottom. Pull the string until it is tight, but without lifting the weight. Use a pen to mark the exact spot on the string where it meets the surface. Lift out the string and the weight. Hold them against a ruler or a yardstick to figure out the depth.

Here, you could have just put the yardstick into the water and gotten the same

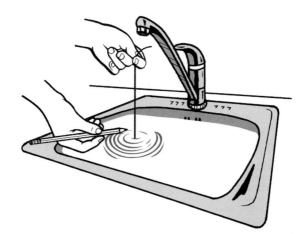

results. But you can't do that for any lake or pool that's more than three feet deep.

Henry sat in a boat to take his pond measurements. If you need a boat or a raft to reach the middle of a lake, *be sure to wear a life jacket and take an adult with you.*

Otherwise, you can sit at the side of a pool. Holding one end of the rope, drop the rope and the weight into the water. Let the weight land on the bottom. Pull the rope tightly, and make your mark at the surface. How easy is it to pull the rope back up? How deep is this water?

Walden Pond from Pine Hill, photographed by Herbert Wendell Gleason.
The Thoreau Institute at Walden Woods

that this result is more inspiring and better for me than if a thousand had bought my wares. It affects my privacy less and leaves me freer." Who needed the problems of celebrity?

Writing *Walden*

But his writing had gained him at least a few fans who were now friends. Teacher Harrison Gray Otis Blake wrote to Henry from Worcester, Massachusetts, after reading one of his essays in the *Dial*. The two became lifelong friends and correspondents. Henry began to visit Worcester to see Blake and another new friend there, tailor Theo Brown. The men held inspiring philosophical conversations whenever they got together. Blake even traveled with Henry to Mount Wachusett and to

Mount Monadnock. He was a more reliable walking companion than Ellery Channing was.

Blake also arranged for his Concord friend to give lectures in Worcester. Following Emerson's example, Thoreau had begun to speak to audiences in some of the cities and towns of New England. Sometimes he spoke about his travels to Cape Cod or to Quebec. Sometimes his topic was the practical art of walking, as he saw it. But most often, he spoke about his time at Walden. People wanted to hear how and why he had chosen to live there.

At first, Thoreau may not have intended to write a book about his two-year experience at the pond. But he gave more than 30 lectures in the nine years after he left, and most of those talks were about Walden. He pulled his notes together and tested some of his material out on his listeners. He emphasized the importance of getting outside and appreciating nature. "Our village life would stagnate if it were not for the unexplored forests and meadows which surround it," he said. "We need the tonic of wildness. . . . We can never have enough of nature."

He also had advice for anyone who heard his story and thought that he or she might try to imitate it. "I would not have any one adopt *my* mode of living on any account," he said. "I desire that there may be as many different persons in the world as possible; but I would have each one be very careful to find out and pursue *his own* way, and not his father's or his mother's or his neighbor's instead. The youth may build or plant or sail, only let him not be hindered from doing that which he tells me he would like to do." Everyone had to find their own paths and make their own choices.

Henry took much time and effort to write his second book. He worked the text through seven complete drafts, all written by hand with pen and ink. Perhaps he thought by concentrating on every detail—giving them as much attention as he gave properties when he surveyed them—*Walden* would become a better book than *A Week* was. He put even more of his philosophies into these pages. And once again, he changed the timeline. He combined his two years into just one that began with summer and ended with the following spring.

English is a dynamic language, with words that can carry different meanings in different situations and can be understood in several different ways. Henry enjoyed finding and using such words in his descriptions. He especially liked to use metaphors and similes to make his readers think about relationships.

A metaphor compares two usually unlike things, often by using the word *is*.

"A lake is the landscape's most beautiful and expressive feature. It is earth's eye; looking into which the beholder measures the depth of his own nature."

"Time is but the stream I go a-fishing in. I drink at it, but while I drink I see the sandy bottom and detect how shallow it is."

"Heaven is under our feet, as well as over our heads."

A simile compares one thing to another, using the word *like*.

"The whistle of the locomotive penetrates my woods summer and winter, sounding like the scream of a hawk sailing over some farmer's yard."
"On gala days the town fires its great guns, which echo like popguns to these woods."
"The finest qualities of our nature, like the bloom on fruits, can be preserved only by the most delicate handling."

Using these tools of language and writing, Henry found connections between what happened in nature and what happened among the people in the town, in the country, in the government, and around the world. As a result, the book *Walden* is about much more than one man's life spent next to a pond.

Walden; or, Life in the Woods was finally published by Ticknor & Fields in August 1854. This time, two thousand copies were printed. And this time, the reviews were more favorable. Although it was not a bestseller, the first run of *Walden* sold out by 1859. The publisher agreed to do a second printing after Henry's death in 1862. *Walden* has not been out of print since then.

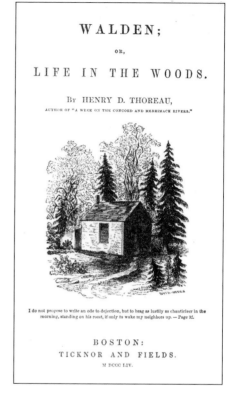

The title page of the first edition of *Walden*, with illustration by Sophia Thoreau.

The Thoreau Institute at Walden Woods

Reading *Walden*

Walden can be a difficult book to read, especially for young people. Students usually wait until they're in high school or college to pick it up. What can you do if you're younger?

One option is to listen to an audio book or to have an adult read it to you. Because Henry wrote most of his essays and parts of his books as lectures first, it's often easier to understand his points when you *hear* them, rather than when you *read* them.

Another suggestion is to select only the chapters that match your own interests.

TOPIC	READ OR LISTEN TO THIS CHAPTER:
Building his house at Walden	"Economy," paragraphs 60–77
Why he lived at Walden	"Where I Lived, and What I Lived For," paragraphs 6–16
Concord's lack of education & culture	"Reading," last 4 paragraphs
Railroads	"Sounds," paragraphs 6–14
Being alone	"Solitude"
Entertaining	"Visitors," paragraphs 1–5
Gardening	"The Bean-Field"
Concord & the jail story	"The Village"
Living at Walden	"The Ponds," paragraphs 1–4
Walden Pond	"The Ponds," paragraphs 5–27
Meeting an Irishman	"Baker Farm"
What we eat & if we should hunt or fish	"Higher Laws"

TOPIC	READ OR LISTEN TO THIS CHAPTER:
A battle of ants	"Brute Neighbors," paragraphs 12–13
Building the chimney	"House-Warming," paragraphs 5–10
Visitors	"Former Inhabitants; and Winter Visitors," paragraphs 14–23
Birds & mammals	"Winter Animals"
Hunters & hunting	"Winter Animals," paragraphs 9–23
Measuring Walden	"The Pond in Winter," paragraphs 6–10
Ice harvesting	"The Pond in Winter," paragraphs 16–21
Spring & the value of nature	"Spring"
Why he left Walden	"Conclusion," paragraphs 4–10
Advice for living	"Conclusion," paragraphs 13–19

Henry wrote in the style of his time, with long sentences and long paragraphs. Sometimes he made puns and made fun of himself. He also quoted pieces of classic literature that even adult readers may not know today. Don't worry about understanding all of the names. Read or listen to the selections as a way to learn about his ideas about nature and life.

Most libraries and library systems own copies of *Walden* and a variety of other books containing Henry's writings. An "annotated edition" of *Walden* will explain the classic references and the most confusing language. You may also find it easier to read books containing just Henry's journal entries or some of his best quotes.

You can read his books, essays, and journals online at: www.walden.org/Library/The_Writings_of_Henry_David_Thoreau:_The_Digital_Collection.

HENRY DAVID THOREAU was imprisoned for one night in a jail on this site, July, 1846 for refusing to recognize the right of the state to collect taxes from him in support of slavery—an episode made famous in his essay "Civil Disobedience".

Marker at the site where Thoreau spent a night in jail and was inspired to write "Civil Disobedience."
Robert DePaolo

CIVIL RIGHTS AND SOCIAL REFORMS

Thoreau paid close attention to more than just the plants, animals, and waterways of New England. He watched what the government and the people around him were doing, too. He wasn't always pleased with what he saw. And he wasn't afraid to speak up or to take action.

He thought that too many folks spent each day mindlessly gliding along, not giving much thought to what they were doing. "The mass of men lead lives of quiet desperation," he wrote. With his writings he saw himself as a kind of rooster, crowing to wake up his sleeping neighbors. "To be awake is to be alive," he said. "As boys are sometimes required to show an excuse for being absent from school, so it seems to me that men should have to show some excuse for being here."

Following His Higher Law

When others blindly accepted a situation, Thoreau was the kind of person who would look at it and think to himself, *Now, wait a minute. Is this right? Is it reasonable?* And when it came to obeying laws, he believed that people had the right to follow their inner instincts and to do what they thought was correct. This was their "higher law."

He didn't mind paying taxes, if they made sense. But he protested when he—like everyone else living in

Henry David Thoreau, 1856. Daguerreotype by Benjamin Maxham of Worcester, Massachusetts.

Concord Free Public Library

Concord—was charged a fee to pay the salary of the minister of First Parish, the only church in town. Thoreau did not attend the church's services. He didn't go to any church. He wrote a letter to the town clerk and asked to be removed from the membership list. The town officials agreed with his request. He was not sent a church bill again.

Although he was a calm and thoughtful person more often than not, Thoreau became a man of action when his passions stirred him. If others considered him a nonconformist, so be it. "If a man does not keep pace with his companions, perhaps it is because he hears a different drummer," he said. "Let him step to the music which he hears, however measured or far away." This was how he had chosen to live his own life.

Under Arrest

One July day in 1846, when Thoreau was still living at Walden, he headed into downtown Concord to pick up a repaired shoe at a cobbler's shop. He was stopped by the sheriff, Sam Staples, who told Thoreau that he owed money to Massachusetts. Every man of voting age had to pay the state poll tax each year in order to be allowed to vote in elections, or to "go to the polls." Thoreau, now age 29, had not paid it for years. He had also never voted. Still, he owed $1.50 for the year, whether he voted or not. It was Sam Staples's job to collect it. Thoreau refused to give it to him.

"I'll pay your tax, Henry, if you're hard up," said Sam. Henry turned him down. Being able to afford the tax wasn't the point. He simply didn't think it applied to him. The sheriff reluctantly arrested him. Henry went quietly with Sam to the Middlesex County jail, which stood at the end of the street and near the town center.

In Thoreau's mind, this tax seemed to have no purpose. School and highway taxes made sense. The money raised went toward maintaining or fixing something specific. But dollars gained from the poll tax could be used for anything. Massachusetts could send the funds to the federal government to help continue to fight the Mexican-American War, which he opposed.

The state could use the funds to find runaway slaves who had come from the South and send them back to their former owners. The Thoreaus were abolitionists who helped slaves find their way north to freedom. Henry didn't want to give any amount of money to a government that would take part in such actions. He felt as though the state was intruding upon his individual rights. Well, he would follow his own higher law in return. Even if it meant going to jail.

The Middlesex County jail was built of granite blocks and stood three stories high. It contained eighteen cells. There were double sets of iron grates at the windows. Iron pickets topped the ten-foot wall surrounding the building. Thoreau must have walked past the place often without giving it much thought. It looked medieval,

Volunteer with a Local Charity

"You must have a genius [a talent] for charity as well as for anything else. As for Doing-good, that is one of the professions which are full. Moreover, I have tried it fairly, and, strange as it may seem, am satisfied that it does not agree with my constitution. . . . But I would not stand between any man and his genius; and to him who does this work, which I decline, with his whole heart and soul and life, I would say, Persevere, even if the world call it doing evil." Thoreau wasn't totally honest when he wrote these words in *Walden*. He may not have donated his free time to the well-meaning organizations of his day, but he did volunteer to help individuals whenever they needed it. He moved into the Emerson household to take care of the family for those months when Ralph Waldo Emerson was away from home. He helped a few runaway slaves move closer to Canada and to freedom. He did the same for Francis Meriam, one of John Brown's men, after the failed raid at Harpers Ferry. In some very difficult situations, Henry quietly did what needed to be done.

The act of "doing-good" not only benefits others, it also gives you personal satisfaction. You can make a difference in your neighborhood—and even beyond it—by volunteering with a local charity.

ADULT SUPERVISION REQUIRED

WHAT YOU NEED TO FIND OUT

- The kinds of tasks you want to do and can do
- The related charities or nonprofit groups in your area

Think about your favorite activities. Would you rather work with people, or animals, or objects (such as books, boxes, bicycles, etc.)? Would you rather work inside a building or outside? Work with your mind, or with your hands? What job would you most like to do someday? Your answers should help you decide what kind of group or site could use your help.

Once you have a general idea about where you would like to volunteer, make a list of your own abilities, too. What related knowledge or experiences have you had? What skills could you offer? Do you take directions well? Can you work in a team? Are you prompt and reliable? Can someone count on you to show up when you are needed? Write down your best qualities so that you can give the list to the group leader.

Find the place. Perhaps you already know one. If not, ask a guidance counselor at school or a local librarian. They may have lists of nonprofit organizations in your area. Some examples include:

→ Animal shelter
→ Art or history museum
→ Church-owned charity shop
→ Food bank or homeless shelter
→ Library
→ Nature center or park
→ Outdoor fund-raising event, like a race or a marathon

Go for it! Contact the organization. Visit its office. Apply for a volunteer job. Explain why you are the perfect person to help behind the scenes.

When the group gives you a chance, do your best work. After all, this experience could lead to a job in the same field someday, if you are interested enough. Good luck!

like something you would see in Europe during the Middle Ages.

But now put into this strange new situation, he paid attention to every detail. "It was like traveling into a far country, such as I had never expected to behold, to lie there for one night," he wrote. "It seemed to me that I never had heard the town clock strike before, nor the evening sounds of the village; for we slept with the windows open, which were inside the grating." He could hear all of the voices and activities from the kitchen of the Middlesex Hotel, which was right next door. "It was a closer view of my native town. I was fairly inside of it. I never had seen its institutions before. . . . I began to comprehend what its inhabitants were about."

In the meantime, the news of Thoreau's arrest had spread. That evening an unidentified person came to the door of the Staples home and delivered Thoreau's tax payment. It was probably Henry's aunt, Maria Thoreau, who lived just steps away from the jail in a large white house that would eventually become part of a hotel.

Sam thought it was then too late in the day to release Henry. He waited until morning to open the cell. Thoreau became angry when he learned that his tax had been paid. He had hoped to bring more attention to the unjust policies of state and local government. But now he wasn't even allowed to stay behind bars. "I was released the next day, obtained my mended shoe, and returned to the woods in season to get my dinner of huckleberries

on Fair Haven Hill." He went back to his house at Walden.

A 1970 play called *The Night Thoreau Spent in Jail* reconstructs this event. The script includes a scene where Ralph Waldo Emerson visits Thoreau's cell. "Henry, what are you doing in jail?" he asks.

Thoreau replies, "Waldo, what are you doing *out* of jail?"

The point is that Thoreau thinks his friend should have taken the same stand against the state. It's a great story, but it isn't true, even though a number of English teachers and other folks still repeat it often. We have no proof that Emerson went to the jail on the night of Thoreau's arrest. The more likely story is that when the two friends next met, Emerson asked Thoreau why he had gone to jail. And Thoreau would have replied, "Why did you not?"

A New Lecture Series

Emerson wasn't the only person who wondered why Thoreau had allowed himself to get arrested. More folks asked Thoreau questions about what happened that day. Out of the experience came two separate but similar lectures he called "The Rights and Duties of the Individual in Relation to the State." He presented them to audiences in Concord in 1848.

Here Thoreau explained the details of his arrest and his night spent in jail. He outlined what he thought the relationship should be between citizens and their government officials. "I think that we should be men first, and subjects afterward," he said. "I ask for, not at once no government, but *at once* a better government. Let every man make known what kind of government would command his respect, and that will be one step toward obtaining it." The United States was set up as a democracy. But did every citizen truly have a say in how it was run? "Is a democracy, such as we know it, the last improvement possible in government?" he wondered. "Is it not possible to take a step further towards recognizing and organizing the rights of man?

As for the people themselves, they had their own responsibilities to consider what was morally right. "There are thousands who are *in opinion* opposed to slavery and to the war, who yet in effect do nothing to put an end to them," he complained. Thoreau was just one person. But at least he had taken a firm stand and had done something that he felt would serve to combat those two challenges. "Even voting *for the right* is *doing* nothing for it," he said. "It is only expressing to men feebly your desire that it should prevail." Sometimes true action was needed instead.

Civil Disobedience

In 1849, his lecture was published in *Aesthetic Papers* as "Resistance to Civil Government." After Thoreau's death, the piece was reprinted and renamed "On the Duty of Civil Disobedience."

Although Thoreau never once used the phrase "civil disobedience," it is a concept that is now firmly associated with him. One dictionary defines the term as "nonviolent opposition to a government policy or law by refusing to comply with it, on the grounds of conscience." Thoreau is credited with encouraging the practice of using passive resistance and nonviolence to protest unjust rules or laws. Over the years his essay has inspired many people, including Indian leader Mohandas Gandhi in the early part of the 20th century and American civil rights leader Martin Luther King Jr. in the 1950s and '60s.

In Thoreau's day, only men could vote in state and federal elections. He chose not to do so. And someone else always paid his annual poll tax. The poll tax remained in effect in Massachusetts and in other states until the 24th Amendment was added to the United States Constitution in 1964. Today American citizens cannot be denied the right to vote "by reason of failure to pay any poll tax or other tax."

Thoreaus for Abolition

By taking a public position against slavery and war, Henry was in truth catching up with his mother and sisters. Cynthia, Helen, and Sophia Thoreau (along with Lidian Emerson, Waldo's wife) had been members of the Concord Female Anti-Slavery Society since it was founded in 1837. They made a point of attending state and national meetings for the cause. At the 1844 New England

Mohandas Gandhi (1869-1948)

Mohandas Gandhi was born in Porbandar, a coastal city located in what was then the British colony of India. He is most known for campaigning for the rights of Indians living in South Africa (1893–1914) and for leading a national Indian movement to gain independence from Great Britain (1915–1947). His followers gave him the title "Mahatma," meaning "Great Soul."

As a young man, Gandhi studied law in London, England. There he had a chance to read a copy of "Civil Disobedience." He found it interesting enough that he searched for more of Thoreau's writings. He read a biography about the American author that had recently been written by Englishman Henry S. Salt.

When Gandhi moved to South Africa to do some legal work, he was shocked by the way his fellow Indians were treated. They were discriminated against because of their dark skin. Inspired by examples set by Thoreau and others, Gandhi began to use the methods of civil disobedience and nonviolence in order to change the situation. He organized a strike among Indian miners. He edited a magazine called *Indian Opinion*. He was arrested multiple times. Gradually, reform happened.

Gandhi had read Thoreau's essays "with great pleasure and equal profit," and he thought Henry's words were "convincing and truthful." He often placed Thoreau quotes and biographical articles about the American author in *Indian Opinion*. He described Thoreau as "a great writer, philosopher, poet, and withal a most practical man, that is, he taught

Portrait of Mohandas K. "Mahatma" Gandhi when he was a young lawyer.
Culver Pictures/The Art Archive at Art Resource, NY

nothing he was not prepared to practice in himself. He was one of the greatest and most moral men America has produced." Gandhi probably knew that Thoreau had read the *Bhagavad Gita* and other Hindu writings. The two shared a common bond.

Gandhi agreed with Thoreau's approach of protesting laws that went against human rights, but he didn't like the words connected to it. He thought "civil disobedience" (a phrase Thoreau never used) and "nonviolence" were negative terms that focused too much on conflict. Gandhi created his own more positive word instead: *satyagraha*. It meant "truth force" or "soul force." It meant doing what you knew in your heart to be true, to be right. This philosophy was similar to the higher law that Thoreau talked about.

Thoreau took his most famous stand as one man, on one day, in one small town in Massachusetts. Gandhi expanded the practice to involve an entire population in an independence movement when he returned to India. It took 32 years for his people to eventually break away from Great Britain and create the separate countries of India and Pakistan. Along the way, Gandhi spent a total of seven years of his life in prison as punishment for his resistance actions.

Just five months after the passage of the Indian Independence Act, Mahatma Gandhi was assassinated by someone who misinterpreted his plans for religious tolerance in India and Pakistan. He was 78 years old.

Both Gandhi and Thoreau, and their actions and words, influenced American civil rights leader Martin Luther King Jr. He wrote: "Mahatma Gandhi never had more than one hundred persons absolutely committed to his philosophy. But with this small group of devoted followers, he galvanized the whole of India, and through a magnificent feat of nonviolence challenged the might of the British Empire and won freedom for his people."

Anti-Slavery Convention in Boston, the Thoreau women voted for a resolution that favored dissolution—a break of the northern states away from the South. Just months before Henry's night in jail in 1846, the women of his household each signed a pledge against the war with Mexico at another antislavery convention. They may not have been able to vote in government-based elections but they could voice their opinions publicly at these large gatherings.

Whenever abolitionists like Frederick Douglass and Harriet Tubman came through Concord to give speeches, the Thoreaus often hosted them overnight in their home. When Henry's sister Helen died of consumption (tuberculosis) in 1849, reformer William Lloyd Garrison wrote a long personal tribute, describing her as a woman of strong convictions, in his antislavery newspaper, the *Liberator*. The Thoreau women eagerly attended group meetings where they listened, learned, talked, and passed resolutions. Henry instead preferred to act as an individual, on his own.

Stories that Henry hid runaway slaves in his small house at Walden are probably untrue. But the Thoreaus gave temporary shelter to at least a few former slaves in their family home in Concord. Henry helped them travel north by delivering each one to a nearby train station. He wrote in his journal on October 1, 1851:

5 p.m. Just put a fugitive slave who has taken the name of Henry Williams into the cars for Canada. He escaped from Stafford County Virginia to Boston last October.... He lodged with us & waited in the house till funds were collected with which to forward him. Intended to dispatch him at noon through to Burlington [Vermont]—but when I went to buy his ticket saw one at the Depot who looked & behaved so much like a Boston policeman, that I did not venture that time.

In spite of the risks, Henry was later able to get Williams on a train. He must have gotten personal satisfaction by helping these folks continue their journeys to freedom.

In the 1850s, Henry spent time writing, surveying, studying nature closely, and making detailed notes and drawings in his journal. But the passage of two national laws got his attention, too.

The first was the Fugitive Slave Law. It required runaway slaves to be caught and returned to their owners even if they were discovered in northern states. Henry spoke against this policy in a lecture called "Slavery in Massachusetts," which he read during a large rally in Framingham, Massachusetts, on July 4, 1854. Once again, he criticized both state and federal authorities, and this time, he did so in front of hundreds of people. "The effect of a good government is to make life more valuable, —of a bad one, to make it less valuable," he said. "A government which deliberately enacts injustice, and persists in it, will at length ever become the laughing-stock of the world."

Martin Luther King Jr. (1929-1968)

Today we remember Dr. Martin Luther King Jr. as a civil rights activist, a minister, and an inspiring speaker and writer. His birthday is celebrated as a national holiday in the United States each January.

Martin Luther King Jr. was born in Atlanta, Georgia, on January 15, 1929. He grew up in a time and a place where public services were divided by race. Black people were not allowed to use the same restaurants, water fountains, or restrooms as white people. This was a situation that King had to deal with on a regular basis.

King left Booker T. Washington High School early, at age fifteen, to enter Morehouse College. He majored in sociology, which is the study of how people act in our society. During his last year at Morehouse (1947–1948), he took a philosophy course that included the reading of "Civil Disobedience." "I was so deeply moved that I reread the work several times," he said. "That was my first intellectual contact with the theory of nonviolent resistance."

In 1950, King listened to a lecture about the nonviolent civil rights work of Mohandas Gandhi in South Africa and India. King found it "profound and electrifying." He quickly bought books by and about Gandhi. To his strong Christian beliefs, he added the inspirational and influential words of both Thoreau and Gandhi.

King went on to earn a divinity degree at Crozer Theological Seminary near Philadelphia and a doctorate in systematic theology at Boston University. His first job was as minister for the Dexter Avenue Baptist Church in Montgomery, Alabama. In that city on December 1, 1955, an African American seamstress and civil rights activist named Rosa Parks was arrested for refusing to give up her bus seat to a white passenger. Montgomery's segregated buses had caused problems for black people in that city for decades. Parks served as the secretary of the local branch of the NAACP, and she had been forced to get off a bus twelve years earlier because she wouldn't follow the white driver's unfair rules. This time, she stayed in her seat and allowed herself to be arrested. Black residents united to rally behind Parks. Dr. King was soon asked to lead the new Montgomery Improvement Association to organize a nonviolent boycott of bus use by African Americans. For weeks, thousands of people helped each other find different ways to get around the city.

King later wrote: "At this point I began to think about Thoreau's *Essay on Civil Disobedience.* I remembered how, as a college student, I had been moved when I first read this work. I became convinced that what we were preparing to do in Montgomery was related to what Thoreau had expressed. We were simply saying to the white community, 'We can no longer lend our cooperation to an evil system.'"

The boycott lasted more than a year. In the end, a Supreme Court decision allowed Montgomery bus passengers of any race to sit wherever they chose. This action marked a successful step toward equal rights for African Americans. It also introduced Martin Luther King Jr. to the country as one of the leaders of a nonviolent civil rights movement.

Dr. King continued to be involved in civil rights campaigns and demonstrations throughout the American South. He spoke to large crowds gathered at the nation's capital during the Prayer Pilgrimage for Freedom (1957) and the March on Washington for Jobs and Freedom (1963). That's when he delivered his famous "I Have a Dream" speech. He once even followed in Gandhi's footsteps and visited India for a month. For all of his efforts, he won the international Nobel Peace Prize in 1964.

Dr. King was helping striking garbage workers in Memphis when he was assassinated on April 4, 1968. Although he had been a civil rights activist for only twelve years, his accomplishments and his spirit of nonviolent protest still live on. They are perhaps even more relevant to us today.

Martin Luther King Jr. addressing a group of followers after their interrupted march in Selma, March 9, 1965.

Kharbine-Tapabor/The Art Archive at Art Resource, NY

Henry took another jab at the voting process too, as he had done when he once talked about his own poll tax arrest. "The fate of the country does not depend on how you vote at the polls—the worst man is as strong as the best at that game; it does not depend on what kind of paper you drop into the ballot-box once a year, but on what kind of man you drop from your chamber into the street every morning." He emphasized that it was up to the citizens themselves to take real action. Just voting and hoping for the best wasn't good enough.

The second troublesome law was the Kansas-Nebraska Act. People who settled in these two new states could decide if they would allow slavery there. As a result, antislavery supporters from the northern states hurried to the plains to try to block the spread of slavery.

John Brown and Kansas

Abolitionist John Brown of Connecticut became a key radical in this Free State movement. He felt so strongly about the evils of slavery that he wasn't against using force to make his point. He and his sons went to Kansas and led some of the bloodiest fighting in the region.

A group of northern men began to give money and supplies to Brown so he could continue his campaign against slavery. These "Secret Six" were Thomas Wentworth Higginson, Samuel Gridley Howe, Theodore Parker, Franklin Sanborn, Gerrit Smith, and George Luther Stearns. Henry

Create a Silhouette

Thoreau wrote this note in his journal on May 26, 1857: "My mother was telling to-night of the sounds which she used to hear summer nights when she was young and lived on the Virginia Road. . . . Says she used to get up at midnight and go and sit on the door-step when all in the house were asleep, and she could hear nothing in the world but the ticking of the clock in the house behind her."

A single silhouette is the only picture we have of Henry's mother, Cynthia Dunbar Thoreau. In it, she's wearing a cap with a small bow on top. In the days before methods of photography were developed, cutting a silhouette was a way of capturing a person's profile. You can try your hand at drawing and cutting a silhouette of someone. In return, you can have your own silhouette drawn and cut, too.

WHAT YOU NEED

- A bright lamp that you can turn or aim
- Black paper
- White paper
- A pencil or a piece of white chalk
- Tape
- Glue
- Scissors
- Black crayon, marker, or paint (optional)

Have a friend sit or stand near a wall, facing to the side. Warn her not to move. Put a lamp beside her and aim its light directly toward her head and neck. Tape black paper onto the wall behind her, exactly where her shadow forms the silhouette.

Trace the outline of her shadow with the pencil or chalk. This could be a tricky task, because you will either have to move between your friend and the wall or lean over her. You'll also have to avoid getting yourself in the way of the outline. Take your time. Do your best to follow the line.

When you are done tracing, take the paper down and cut along the line with scissors. To finish off the bottom—where the rest of the person's body would be—cut an artistic curve. Glue the black silhouette in the middle of a white sheet of paper. Write the person's name and the date at the bottom, and sign your work.

Trade places! Ask your friend to draw and cut your silhouette next.

Option: If you do not have black paper, you can use a sheet of white paper instead.

After you draw the outline, you can fill in the silhouette with a black crayon or marker or even with dark paint. No cutting will be necessary. You may use up a lot of ink, though.

Silhouette of Cynthia Dunbar Thoreau, 1804–1806, attributed to artist William King. *Concord Museum, www.concordmuseum.org*

Thoreau knew most of them. He was closest to Frank Sanborn, a teacher and writer who lived in Concord and who often ate lunch at the Thoreau house. As a result, Thoreau had a chance to meet John Brown when he came through Massachusetts to visit his supporters. After finding too many people who were mostly talk and little action, Thoreau admired John Brown for his commitment to the cause. He gave Brown "a trifling" amount of money as a donation.

Not many knew what Brown had been planning. On October 16, 1859, he and his small army of 21 men attacked the federal armory in Harpers Ferry, Virginia. They had hoped to steal weapons and ammunition in order to give them to southern slaves to help them manage escapes. Instead, the group was stopped by soldiers. Ten of Brown's men were killed, including two of his sons. Five men had escaped. Seven were captured and arrested, including Brown, who was wounded. He was charged with treason and slave insurrection and was sentenced to death.

As soon as this news reached Concord, it was the main talk around town. Thoreau began filling his journal with his reactions. "It galls me to listen to the remarks of craven-hearted neighbors who speak disparagingly of Brown because he resorted to violence, resisted the government, threw his life away!—what way have they thrown their lives, pray?" He still admired the man for taking action.

He wrote a speech called "A Plea for Captain John Brown," which he read to audiences in

Kansas and Nebraska

Kansas would eventually become a free state in January 1861. By then, eight southern slaveholding states had seceded from the union. The country was just months away from the beginning of the Civil War. Nebraska's statehood came in 1867, several years after the war ended.

Concord, Boston, and Worcester just a few weeks later. He portrayed Brown as a hero. "He had the courage to face his country herself, when she was in the wrong," he said. "No man in America has ever stood up so persistently and effectively for the dignity of human nature, knowing himself for a man, and the equal of any and all governments. In that sense he was the most American of us all."

Thoreau was normally a pacifist, a peaceable man. Thinking about John Brown's violent tactics caused Thoreau to realize something about himself: "I do not wish to kill nor to be killed, but I can foresee circumstances in which both these things would be by me unavoidable." Such means might be necessary to achieve a moral goal.

When John Brown was hanged on December 2, 1859, Thoreau was one of the speakers at the memorial service held in the Concord town hall. His lecture was later published in the *Liberator* as "The Last Days of John Brown." Once again, he described the man as a hero.

John Brown.
Art Resource, NY

I never hear of any particularly brave and earnest man, but my first thought is of John Brown, and what relation he may be to him. I meet him at every turn. He is more alive than ever he was. He has earned immortality. He is not confined to North Elba [New York, Brown's home] nor to Kansas. He is no longer working in secret. He works in public, and in the clearest light that shines on this land.

Francis Meriam, one of the men who had escaped from the scene at Harpers Ferry, showed up unexpectedly at Frank Sanborn's house on the night of Brown's death. This was a risky situation. Sanborn and the other members of the Secret Six were in some trouble themselves. Authorities were searching for anyone who had ties to John Brown. Having Meriam at his home would make matters worse for Sanborn. He quickly got permission to borrow Emerson's horse and wagon. He asked Thoreau to drive Meriam to the railroad station in South Acton, the next town to the west, so Meriam could make his way to Canada. Thoreau did this favor the next morning and put Meriam on the train. In this small, secondhand way, he helped the hero he had been writing and talking about.

These months of focusing on John Brown and the Harpers Ferry aftermath had taken Thoreau away from his time with nature. It was a jolt for him to realize that the world had continued to turn, and that fall had changed into winter. He gradually returned to his natural studies during the next year. He was especially interested in learning how plants regenerated themselves by using their seeds, and how species of trees succeeded one another over time.

But even as he walked through the neighboring fields and woodlands in search of answers, Thoreau also witnessed the tensions growing throughout America. So much had already happened: the many antislavery meetings that the Thoreau women attended; the failed mission of John Brown; his own small acts and lectures. These efforts and many others brought publicity, but they didn't put an end to the practice of slavery in the southern states. It would take Abraham Lincoln and a four-year-long civil war to do that.

Henry lived through only the first year of the war. He didn't have the chance to see how these conflicts would be resolved.

Write to a News Editor or Elected Official

"The greatest compliment that was ever paid me was when one asked what I thought, and attended to my answer. I am surprised, as well as delighted, when this happens, it is such a rare use he would make of me." Thoreau expressed his opinions in his public lectures and written essays. In fact, he wrote this remark in a lecture called "What Shall It Profit?" that became the essay, "Life Without Principle."

You may not have the chance to give a speech or to publish a piece of writing on your own. Instead, you can use one of the two traditional outlets for expressing your opinion on an issue: writing either to a news editor or to an elected official. These people look for input from their readers and residents.

ADULT SUPERVISION REQUIRED

WHAT YOU NEED TO FIND OUT

- An issue or situation that you feel strongly about
- The best way to contact the editor or official (by e-mail, online form, or written letter)

First, decide upon an issue or a situation that affects you. Is there something wrong in your neighborhood that you believe needs to be made right? Here's your opportunity to talk about it. The sky's the limit!

Next, write your thoughts down on paper or in a document on a computer. Describe the issue. Explain your concerns. Offer your opinions and a solution, if you have one. Be polite! Your words could very well be made public. Say what you need to say in fewer than 250 words. Sign the letter with your first name only and include your age or grade in school. Read your work aloud to yourself and to friends to make sure that it sounds good. Have someone else check your grammar, spelling, and punctuation.

With the help of an adult, look online for contact information. If you want to send your letter to a news editor, you should find guidelines on the newspaper website under the heading "Opinion" or "Letters to the Editor." If you are searching an elected official's site, look for "Contact Me." The official could be anyone, ranging from the president of the country to members of the board who manage your local town, township, or school.

In both cases, let an adult follow the posted instructions. If he sends your letter through e-mail or an online form, he will have to include his street address, phone number, and e-mail address. Or you can print your letter and send it through the mail.

Don't worry if you don't get a response right away. If the news editor is interested in printing your letter, the office will call the sender to get his permission. Then your work will be published for everyone to see. An elected official will often have a staff member respond via e-mail within a few days. The reply will probably include a long statement summarizing the official's opinions on the issue you raised.

Congratulations on voicing your opinion!

Henry David Thoreau's signature.
The Thoreau Institute at Walden Woods

Mount Wachusett today.

Robert M. Young

4

EXPLORING NEW ENGLAND'S MOUNTAINS

In the 19th century, Concord's landscape was made up mostly of farms and fields. But its terrain was not entirely flat. Some low hills gave the earth more variety. Thoreau was naturally drawn to these places. "One must needs climb a hill to know what a world he inhabits," he said, as he sat on a rock on Nawshawtuct. He overlooked the spot where the Assabet and Sudbury Rivers meet to form the Concord. "Thus I admire the grandeur of my emerald carriage, with its border of blue, in which I am rolling through space."

Mount Wachusett

From the top of one of these hills, Thoreau could clearly see the dark blue outline of Mount Wachusett on the western horizon. The mountain stood more than 2,000 feet above sea level and lay about 30 miles away in Worcester County. It is still a landmark for people living and traveling in central Massachusetts.

The sight of Wachusett must have been too enticing for Thoreau to resist. He and his friend Richard Fuller decided to walk to the mountain in the summer of 1842. It took them two days, July 19–20, to reach the summit.

"Wachusett from Fair Haven Hill looks like this: —the dotted line being the top of the surrounding forest." —Henry Thoreau, Journal, August 2, 1852

The Thoreau Institute at Walden Woods

The New England mountains that Thoreau explored.

Corinne H. Smith

Katahdin
∧

Washington
∧
∧
Lafayette

Monadnock
∧

The Catskills
∧∧∧
∧ ∧

Greylock
∧

Wachusett
∧
• Concord

"As we passed through the open country," Thoreau said, "we inhaled the fresh scent of every field, and all nature lay passive, to be viewed and travelled." Eventually the heat of the afternoon sun drove Thoreau and Fuller into finding routes that were shaded by woods. They looked for creeks, too. "We refreshed ourselves by bathing our feet in every rill that crossed the road," Thoreau said. They stayed overnight at an inn located along the Sterling–Princeton town line.

The next morning, the two men hiked the final four miles up the mountainside. When they reached the top, Thoreau first examined the plant life. "The summit consists of a few acres, destitute of trees, covered with bare rocks, interspersed with blueberry bushes, raspberries, gooseberries, strawberries, moss, and a fine wiry grass," he said.

He and Fuller scaled a five-foot stone outpost to get a wider view. Now they could see in every direction. To the east lay the countryside they had hiked across. Concord was out there, somewhere. To the north, west, and south stood some of New England's highest mountains. "Wachusett is, in fact, the observatory of the State," Thoreau said. "There lay Massachusetts, spread out before us in its length and breadth, like a map.

There was the level horizon, which told of the sea on the east and south, the well-known hills of New Hampshire on the north, and the misty summits of the Hoosac and Green Mountains, . . . blue and unsubstantial, like some bank of clouds which the . . . wind would dissipate, on the northwest and west."

One mountain in particular held his attention. "Monadnock, rearing its masculine front in the northwest, is the grandest feature. . . . That New Hampshire bluff,—that promontory of a State,— [with shadows] lowering day and night on this our State of Massachusetts, will longest haunt our dreams."

He and Richard camped overnight on top of Wachusett. When night fell, the dark but star-filled sky was soon lit up by a nearly full moon. The men could see clearly enough to read by moonlight, and they could walk around the summit without stumbling. They may have felt as if they were standing—and then, sleeping—on top of the world.

The next morning, they had a special seat to watch the day break. "At length we saw the sun rise up out of the sea, and shine on Massachusetts; and from this moment the atmosphere grew more and more transparent till the time of our departure, and we began to realize the extent of the view, and how the earth, in some degree, answered to the heavens in breadth, the white villages to the constellations in the sky." Unfortunately, it was time to start for home. Thoreau and Fuller headed back downhill and retraced their steps to Lancaster. Within a few days, they were both back with their families.

Thoreau was impressed enough with his experience that he wrote an essay about it. "A Walk to Wachusett" was published in the magazine *Boston Miscellany of Literature* in January 1843. Included was an original poem. With these rhymes, Thoreau said he had something in common with Wachusett: they both stood alone. And yet, he also felt a connection or a kinship with the mountain:

But special I remember thee,
Wachusett, who like me
Standest alone without society.
Thy far blue eye,
A remnant of the sky,
Seen through the clearing or the gorge,
Or from the windows on the forge,
Doth leaven all it passes by,
Nothing is true,
But stands 'tween me and you,
Thou western pioneer,
Who know'st not shame nor fear,
By venturous spirit driven,
Under the eaves of heaven,
And can'st expand thee there,
And breathe enough of air?
Upholding heaven, holding down earth,
Thy pastime from thy birth,
Not steadied by the one, nor leaning on
  the other;
May I approve myself thy worthy
  brother!

Thoreau returned to Wachusett only once, in October 1854. This time, he used a different way of reaching it. By that time a system of railroads had been built across Massachusetts and much of the northeastern United States. Thoreau rode by train for 35 miles, from Concord to the town of Westminster. Then he walked the remaining four miles south to the mountaintop. This time he was joined by his friends Harrison Gray Otis Blake and Thomas Cholmondeley. And this time, he carried a spyglass with him. Now he could get a better view from the Wachusett summit. He could not only see just the details of the countryside and the other peaks in the region, but he could also turn his eyes to the east and toward the state capital of Boston, 40 miles away. "With a glass you can see vessels in Boston Harbor from the summit, just north of the Waltham hills," Thoreau wrote. Who would have guessed that you could see the outlines of ship masts from that distance?

But it had been his first walking trip and his view of Monadnock from Wachusett that seems to have triggered Thoreau's fascination with all of the mountains in New England—or at least, with as many of them as he could reach within a few days of traveling from home. Over the next 18 years, he climbed some of the tallest ones.

Henry Thoreau's spyglass.
Concord Museum, www.concordmuseum.org

53

Mount Monadnock

In geology, a "monadnock" is a rocky hill or mountain that stands alone and is not part of a range. Mount Wachusett in central Massachusetts happens to be a monadnock. So is Mount Monadnock in southern New Hampshire, which is where the name originated. Standing at 3,165 feet above sea level, Monadnock is more than a thousand feet taller than Wachusett. Today it is one of the most climbed mountains in the world, along with Mount Fuji in Japan and Mount Tai in China.

Monadnock must have been Thoreau's favorite mountain. He visited it four times. His first trip came during the summer of 1844, when he walked by himself around large portions of Massachusetts and New Hampshire. Few notes remain in his journal about the experience. He did camp for at least one night on Monadnock's summit. The next day, he hiked down the mountain and continued on his journey.

When Thoreau returned to the mountain again for several days in 1852, 1858, and 1860, the circumstances were different. Each time, he jotted down the names of the plants, birds, and insects that he saw as well as what the rocks looked like and which paths he had taken. Each time either Ellery Channing or H. G. O. Blake accompanied him; they camped together on the mountain. And each time the men traveled first by train to a nearby station, and then hiked up to Monadnock from there. That way, they could reach the summit quickly and could spend more time exploring the area.

The friends had much to find here, too. A mountain like Monadnock can be deceptive. From a distance, it appears to have only one peak or top ridge. But when you venture closer and actually hike up one of its sides, you find out that this is not the case. "When you are on the mountain, the different peaks and ridges appear more independent; indeed, there is a bewildering variety of ridge and valley and peak," Thoreau said. It's easy for someone to get turned around. The land has steep angles, and the rocks and evergreens tend to look the same. "We lost the path coming down," he wrote in June 1858. "For nothing is easier than to lose your way here, where so little trail is left upon the rocks, and the different rocks and ravines are so much alike. Perhaps no other equal area is so bewildering in this respect as a rocky mountain-summit, though it has so conspicuous a central point."

Thoreau and his friends almost always were rewarded for their efforts by finding ripe berries to pick and eat, however. He was pleased to report in September 1852 that the train had returned him to Concord, "four hours from the time we were picking blueberries on the mountain, with the plants of the mountain fresh in my hat." He could enjoy being in two of his favorite places in just one day, thanks to the efficiency of the railroads.

But they hadn't been up there alone. Monadnock attracted a lot of visitors. "One noon, when I

Gain a Higher View

"The universe is wider than our views of it," Thoreau wrote. He searched for places where he could see over the trees and houses and could look out across the countryside. He enjoyed seeing familiar landscapes—turned slightly stranger—from the views he gained by standing on the crest of a hill or a mountain.

You should be able to find several outside overlooks in your neighborhood, city, and state. You too can get a wider and higher view of your part of the world.

ADULT SUPERVISION REQUIRED

WHAT YOU NEED

- Journal and pen or pencil
- Camera
- Perhaps a bit of courage

Find a way or a place where you can get to a higher elevation. You could step up a ladder, climb a tree, walk or hike to the peak of a hill or mountain, or walk or ride to the top floor of a multistory building. If you are truly climbing, then take all necessary safety precautions. Here the method is not as important as the goal of reaching a summit.

Once you have arrived at the top, look around in every direction. Use as many of your senses as possible. What do you see, smell, hear, touch, or even taste? What can you see now that you couldn't see from below? What landmarks (such as church steeples or taller buildings) do you recognize? Can you spot your own home? What places are now out of sight? How do you feel up here? Do you sense a connection to the earth or to the sky? Which one seems closer?

Stay here for at least an hour. Be sure to write down your thoughts and experiences in your journal. Take some photos to remind yourself of the view later. But be aware that the flat image will never give you the same three-dimensional perspective that your own eyes can show you in person. Be awake and alive in the moment.

Some people are afraid of heights. This fear is called acrophobia. You may be able to step only a few feet up a ladder. You may find it easier to look out of a window of a five-story building than to stand on an open hillside. Or even these views may be challenging for you. It's OK to feel this way. This activity offers you a chance to discover your own comfort levels and possible limitations. Do your best to go outdoors, where you can turn your attention to nature without having to worry about being scared. If you have to stay indoors, then venture as high as you can. The scenery will still be slightly different than what you see every day.

What are the tallest points in your neighborhood, your county, and your state? Are they natural (like hills or mountains), or are they man-made (like buildings or bridges)? Can you visit them all?

was on the top, I counted forty men, women, and children around me, and more were constantly arriving while others were going," Henry wrote. "Certainly more than one hundred ascended it in a day. . . . The mountain was not free of them

Herbert W. Gleason sits in "Thoreau's seat" on Monadnock. From Elizabeth Weston Timlow's *The Heart of Monadnock, 1922*.
From the author's collection

from sunrise to sunset, though most of them left about 5 p.m." He wondered about their motives, though, and he could be critical. Thoreau crested mountains in order to discover interesting wildlife, to look out over the countryside, and to have a spiritual experience. Not everyone followed his example. "It is remarkable what haste the visitors make to get to the top of the mountain and then look away from it," he wrote. "They who simply climb to the peak of Monadnock have seen but little of the mountain. I came not to look *off from* it, but to look *at* it." He inventoried the plants and animals that he saw here, and he compared his sightings from previous trips. He approached Monadnock from both a scientific and a spiritual point of view.

Perhaps the others didn't even pay attention to the fog that often lay in the valleys below. Or they didn't see how little clouds seemed bent on "forming and dissolving" just overhead, as if they "had been attracted by the summit." Thoreau watched and studied these bits of moisture and their interactions with Monadnock. And when they cleared away, he could look around and identify a number of the other peaks of New England. In August 1860, he turned toward the west and wrote: "I never saw a mountain that looked so high and so melted away at last cloud-like into the sky, as Saddleback this eve. . . . If you had first rested your eye on *it*, you would have seen it for a cloud, it was so incredibly high in the sky." And yet, it was indeed a mountain. At 3,491 feet above sea level, it was the tallest one in Massachusetts.

What was in Thoreau's Knapsack?

When Thoreau returned home from Monadnock in August 1860, he listed in his journal all of the items that he had taken on the trip. He especially considered the food provisions, and he noted what changes he would make for his next mountain excursion. Unfortunately, this would be his last one.

I carried on this excursion the following articles (beside what I wore), viz.: —

One shirt.
One pair socks.
Two pocket handkerchiefs.
One thick waistcoat.
One flannel shirt (had no occasion to use it).
India-rubber coat.
Three bosoms [garment that covered the chest].

Towel and soap.
Pins, needles, thread.
A blanket (would have been more convenient if stitched up in the form of a bag).
Cap for the night.
Map and compass.
Spy-glass and microscope and tape.
Saw and hatchet.
Plant-book [press] and blotting-paper.

Paper and stamps.
Botany [manual].
Insect and lichen boxes.
Jack-knife.
Matches.
Waste paper and twine.
Iron spoon and pint dipper with handle.
All in a knapsack.
Umbrella.

N. B. —Add to the above next time a small bag, which may be stuffed with moss or the like for a pillow.

For provision for one, six days, carried: —

2 ½ lbs. of salt beef and tongue.
18 hard-boiled eggs.
2 ½ lbs. sugar and a little salt.
About ¼ lb. of tea.
2 lbs. home-made bread and a piece of cake.

Take only salt beef next time 2 to 3 lbs.
Omit eggs.
2 lbs. of sugar would have done.
⅔ as much would have done.
The right amount of bread, but might have taken more home-made and more solid sweet cake.

N.B. —Carry salt (or some of it) in a wafer-box. Also some sugar in a small box.

Unlike today's hikers, Thoreau didn't have access to power bars, trail mix or gorp, or athletic drinks to give him extra energy to climb over granite boulders on steep mountain paths. He satisfied his sweet tooth by taking along a loaf of sugar. He also foraged for berries along the trail and relied on running brooks for drinking water.

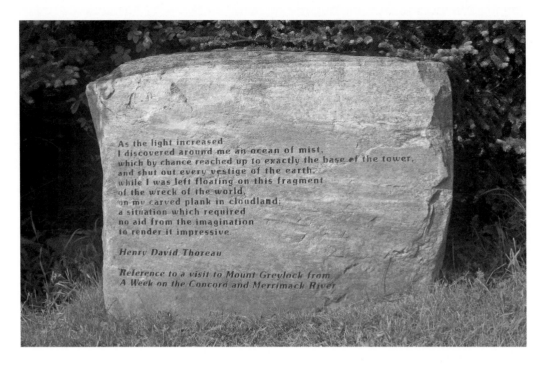

As the light increased
I discovered around me an ocean of mist,
which by chance reached up to exactly the base of the tower,
and shut out every vestige of the earth,
while I was left floating on this fragment
of the wreck of the world,
on my carved plank in cloudland;
a situation which required
no aid from the imagination
to render it impressive.

Henry David Thoreau

Reference to a visit to Mount Greylock from
A Week on the Concord and Merrimack River

A Thoreau quote on a rock
at the top of Mount Greylock
today.

Sylvia G. Buck

Mount Greylock (Saddleback) and the Catskills

After Thoreau first climbed down from Monadnock in 1844, he continued walking. He moved west and south, following the valleys of the Connecticut and Deerfield Rivers into western Massachusetts. He eventually made his way across the Hoosac Range and into the town of North Adams. Saddleback, now known more often as Mount Greylock, rose just to the south.

"I had come over the hills on foot and alone in serene summer days, plucking the raspberries by the way-side, and occasionally buying a loaf of bread at a farmer's house, with a knapsack on my back, which held a few traveller's books and a change of clothing, and a staff in my hand," Thoreau wrote. "Putting a little rice and sugar and a tin cup into my knapsack at this village, I began in the afternoon to ascend the mountain. . . . It seemed a road for the pilgrim to enter upon who would climb to the gate of heaven.

"I reached the summit, just as the sun was setting. Several acres here had been cleared, and were covered with rocks and stumps, and there was a rude observatory in the middle which overlooked the woods. I had one fair view of the country before the sun went down." Thoreau dug a small well to get water, then built a campfire to cook a dinner of rice. The night grew chilly, and he had no thick blanket to sleep under. Instead, he used a few stray boards from the observatory tower building to cover himself. If he was uncomfortable with this odd arrangement, he didn't admit it when he described the incident later.

Before night fell, he caught a glimpse of Williamstown, home of Williams College, down in the valley. This summit observatory belonged to the school. Thoreau liked this idea. "It would really be no small advantage if every college were thus located at the base of a mountain," he wrote. Students could learn much about nature, science, and life in general, in such an environment. By contrast: the campus of Harvard College, his alma mater, sat on the flat plain of the Charles River. There were no mountains in sight.

When Thoreau woke up the next morning, he found that he was suddenly sailing on "an ocean of mist." Clouds billowed below the mountain, obscuring his view of the countryside. It was as if the everyday world below no longer existed. "There was not a crevice left through which the trivial places we name Massachusetts, or Vermont, or New York, could be seen, while I still inhaled the clear atmosphere of a July morning, —if it were July there. All around beneath me was spread for a hundred miles on every side, as far as the eye could reach, an undulating country of clouds, answering in the varied swell of its surface to the terrestrial world it veiled. It was such a country as we might see in dreams, with all the delights of paradise." Perhaps he had stumbled upon that imagined "gate of heaven" he thought he had been climbing toward. But he couldn't stay here. He had agreed to meet Ellery Channing and do more exploring.

Luckily, the previous day he had spied on the southwestern horizon the outlines of their planned destination, the Catskill Mountains of New York. There he "might hope to climb to heaven again." Henry hiked down from Greylock and into a rainy, dreary day. He made his way to Pittsfield and boarded a train heading west toward the Hudson River. (A few years later, author Herman Melville would buy a house in Pittsfield and would look out of his study window at the whale-like ridge of Greylock as he wrote his book, *Moby-Dick*.)

Channing joined him in Pittsfield. The two men transferred to a boat to continue their trek south to the Catskills. Neither one wrote much about this part of their journey. They got at least as far as Kaaterskill Falls, a popular tourist attraction located west of the town of Catskill. By this time, Thoreau had been camping out on his own for more than a week, and he had probably slept in his clothes each night. He looked so disheveled that a passenger on the boat mistook him for a deckhand. Thoreau and Channing soon returned via riverboat and railroad to Concord.

Mount Katahdin

Thoreau was living at Walden Pond in the late summer of 1846 when he decided to travel to Maine. He planned to climb Mount Katahdin, which he called "Ktaadn." At 5,268 feet above sea level, Katahdin is the highest peak in Maine and is the sixth highest peak in New England. By this time, Thoreau had already scaled Washington, Wachusett, Monadnock, and Greylock. Here was his chance at another and different mountain experience.

His cousin Rebecca Billings Thatcher lived in Bangor, Maine, with her husband George, who worked as a lumber agent. George was interested in looking at some property in Katahdin's direction, and he invited Henry to go along on the trip. Thoreau reached their house by taking a steamboat from Boston. The two men proceeded by horse and carriage north along the Penobscot River. They continued along the west branch of the river on foot and in a bateau, a flat-bottomed rowboat, paddled by two expert river men who

Take a Half-Day Hike

"Two or three hours' walking will carry me to as strange a country as I expect ever to see," Henry wrote. He wasn't talking about actually crossing any international borders, of course. He meant instead that he could discover interesting sights and situations and people just by traveling a short distance away from home and by paying attention to what he found.

You can get the same experience by hiking along an established trail or by walking a few miles around your town, city, or county. The possibilities are endless, and the choices are yours.

ADULT SUPERVISION REQUIRED

WHAT YOU NEED

- 🌱 Sturdy shoes
- 🌱 Appropriate clothing for the weather
- 🌱 Journal and pen or pencil
- 🌱 Camera
- 🌱 Packed lunch, with snacks and water
- 🌱 Small garbage bag
- 🌱 Map of the area
- 🌱 Walking stick (optional)
- 🌱 Binoculars (optional)
- 🌱 Compass (optional)
- 🌱 Cell phone, turned OFF (optional; to be turned ON only in an emergency)

Choose the place and the route where you will hike. You could start at your home and just begin walking. You could go to a local nature center, a state park, or a national park, or any other site where official hiking trails have been established. Or you could find a national trail system that ventures even farther: the Appalachian Trail, the Pacific Crest Trail, or another route that comes close to your city or region. Your goals are to get outside, to get walking, and to be aware of what you begin to see around you. The exercise, the destination, and the total number of miles are bonuses. Your experience is what really counts.

Henry preferred to "saunter"—to take his time and savor the outdoors. He also preferred to have companions who didn't chat about the issues of daily life while sauntering. Try to talk with your fellow walkers only about what you are seeing. You don't have to be in motion the whole time. Stop, look, listen, smell. Use as many of your senses as possible. Find a nice place to sit and eat lunch. Take some photos. Be sure to write down your thoughts and experiences in your journal.

Stay outside for as much of the day as possible. If you can, choose a path or trail laid out in a loop. Thoreau preferred this kind of route so that he didn't see the same scenery on his way back home. Take a bag along to pack up your own trash as well as to pick up any pieces of litter you may see along the way.

You may want to coordinate your hike with the American Hiking Society's National Trails Day, which falls on the first Saturday in June. National Get Outdoors Day is June 14. But you can take walks and hikes at any time of the year, and in almost any kind of weather, as long as you are prepared. Can you make it a regular activity? Can you go hiking and exploring at least once a month?

had joined them. This was a remote country, where few people lived or ventured. "The only roads were of Nature's making, and the few houses were camps," Thoreau said. "No face welcomed us but the fine fantastic sprays of free and happy evergreen trees, waving one above another in their ancient home."

Days later, when the group finally made camp near the southern base of the mountain, Thoreau couldn't wait. He climbed up—"and I mean to lay some emphasis on this word *up*"—the steep slope as if it were "a giant's stairway," rattling over rocks and roots and small but sturdy evergreens, their growth stunted by high winds and rough weather. He followed a streambed but didn't get too far. He realized a sense of the climb's challenges, however, before he turned around and returned to his friends for the night. "The mountain seemed a vast aggregation of loose rocks, as if sometime it had rained rocks." How would he achieve his goal this time?

Determined, the next day Thoreau once again approached Katahdin first, and his companions could barely keep up with him. The hiking was rough, the terrain was confusing, and the clouds moved in to further obscure and distort the scene. Katahdin has several peaks, making it difficult for someone to know, even on a clear day, if he has really reached the summit. Comparing his descriptions to present-day maps and knowledge, it is believed that Thoreau must have stopped on a plateau at about 3,800 feet. He did not crest Katahdin, although he was historically one of the few white men known to have attempted it by then. His companions stayed closer to camp and didn't bother to make the climb. Nevertheless, he found the experience itself exhilarating.

First of all, there was the view. From previous mountain summits, Thoreau had been able to spot church steeples, college buildings, roads, and other faint marks of human civilization. Not here. Not in northern Maine. All he saw were trees and lakes. "There it was, the State of Maine, which we had seen on the map, but not much like that. Immeasurable forest for the sun to shine on. . . . No clearing, no house. It did not look as if a solitary traveller had cut so much as a walking-stick there. . . . Countless lakes . . . and mountains also, whose names, for the most part, are known only to the Indians." It was impressive. And also a little scary.

This sight brought with it a feeling of coming face-to-face with an ultimate wildness. Back home and on his other explorations, Thoreau felt comfortable in natural areas like forests and swamps. He admired both wildness and wilderness. He craved them. Katahdin had enormous and raw amounts of both. The mountain showed Thoreau a picture of what the world could have been like before mankind arrived:

It is difficult to conceive of a region uninhabited by man. We habitually presume his presence and influence everywhere. And yet we have not seen pure Nature, unless we have seen her thus vast, and drear, and inhuman. . . .

Nature was here something savage and awful, though beautiful. I looked with awe at the ground I trod on, to see what the Powers had made there, the form and fashion and material of their work. This was that Earth of which we have heard, made out of Chaos and Old Night. Here was no man's garden. . . . It was not lawn, nor pasture, nor mead, nor woodland, nor lea, nor arable, nor waste-land. It was the fresh and natural surface of the planet Earth, as it was made forever and ever.

He was still overwhelmed by Katahdin when he later sat down to write his essay about the encounter. "Think of our life in nature, —daily to be shown matter, to come in contact with it, —rocks, trees, wind on our cheeks! the *solid* earth! the *actual* world! the *common sense! Contact! Contact! Who* are we? *where* are we?" It may have been frightening for Thoreau to come this close to nature. But he didn't allow his quick emotions to put an end to his outdoor explorations. He still had more mountains to climb. His minutes near the top of Katahdin were life-changing ones. They gave him further insights into the wider dimensions of the natural world.

Thoreau went back to Maine twice. He probably had hopes of returning to Katahdin and of finally reaching its summit in triumph someday. But his expeditions of 1853 and 1857 followed the paths of wild rivers and lakes instead of any trails

that would lead to the great mountain, which always loomed in the distance. He did climb Mount Kineo (1,808 ft.) at Moosehead Lake on his third trip. He also shared some of his experiences, including those on Katahdin, in public lectures that he turned into published essays and eventually, into a three-part book.

But he also learned that the act of climbing mountains required much private thought and personal reflection afterward. A few months after his last Maine trip, Thoreau summed up his feelings in a letter to Blake: "Going up there and being blown on is nothing. We never do much climbing while we are there, but we eat our luncheon, etc., very much as at home. It is after we get home that we really get over the mountain, if

The Maine wilderness, as photographed by Herbert W. Gleason.
The Thoreau Institute at Walden Woods

Bake Trail Cakes

"A man may use as simple a diet as the animals, and yet retain health and strength," Thoreau said. He always took along a variety of breads and cakes on his hikes. He variously described these as *"hard bread,"* *"home-made bread,"* *"sweet cakes,"* and *"moist and rich plum cake."* We don't know exactly what this food was. But it had to last for at least several days' worth of hiking.

You can bake bread-like cakes that will not get stale or require refrigeration. Today's historical re-enactors use a similar recipe to make trail bread. Baking it in cupcake form will make it even more portable.

ADULT SUPERVISION REQUIRED

WHAT YOU NEED

- 1 cup of cornmeal
- 1 cup of white flour
- 1 cup of whole wheat flour
- 2 cups of honey (16 fluid ounces)
- Blueberries (optional)
- Mixing bowl and spoon
- Cooking pot or microwave container
- Foil or paper baking cups
- Muffin tin or cookie sheet
- Clean toothpicks

Preheat the oven to 350°F. Mix the three dry flour ingredients together in a bowl. Put the honey in a cooking pot on the stove or in a container in a microwave, and warm it separately for a few minutes. When you can stir the honey easily, pour it into the flour bowl. Mix thoroughly. The batter will get quite thick. If it does not drop easily from a spoon when fully mixed, stir in up to one-quarter cup of hot water to thin the batter.

Option: After mixing the batter, drop two handfuls (about one-half dry pint) of fresh blueberries on top of it. Stir lightly, but not hard enough to break the skins of the berries.

Put baking cups into a muffin tin or onto a flat cookie sheet. Fill each one about three-quarters full of the batter. The cakes will rise only slightly. Place the tin or sheet in the oven. Bake for 16–20 minutes at 350°F. Test the cakes by pushing a toothpick down into one or two of them. If it comes back up with liquid batter still attached, the cakes need to stay in the oven for another minute or two.

You can make 20–24 bread-cakes with this recipe. They will be chewy, and they will stay fresh without refrigeration. You can take them on your half-day hikes and on other outdoor adventures.

ever. What did the mountain say? What did the mountain do?" We may never know what Mount Katahdin really said and did with Thoreau.

Mount Washington and the White Mountains

Thoreau's last lengthy mountain trip came in July 1858, when he and Edward Hoar traveled by carriage to the White Mountains of northern New Hampshire. They intended to study the special plants that grew at those high altitudes. Thoreau also wanted another go at Mount Washington (6,288 ft.), the tallest peak in New England. His first visit to its summit had been in 1839, as part of his two-week boating expedition with his brother John. He had already seen the other spectacular mountains that could be climbed here, too.

Much had changed in the 19 years that had passed, however. The railroad now brought more tourists to the region. New hotels had been built. A new road for carriages was being planned. A man named Sylvester Marsh thought he could construct a rail system with cogs to draw cars and people up one of the steep sides of Mount Washington. Taking a mountain holiday was becoming a popular pastime for those folks who could afford it, and local businessmen were making it easier for travelers to do so.

Thoreau and Hoar spent more than two weeks exploring the heights of New Hampshire. Along the way, they stopped to climb Red Hill (2,029 ft.) in Moultonborough, where they could

get a terrific view of Lake Winnipesaukee, the largest lake in the state. But Thoreau also turned to look toward the northeast, where he saw more enticing peaks: the Sandwich Mountains, the Ossipee, Chocorua, and the White Mountains beyond. They were "lofty and bare, and filling the whole northerly horizon." He thought he even caught a glimpse of his old friend Monadnock, more than 60 miles to the southwest,

The White Mountains, including Mount Washington, from "The White Mountains," in *Harper's New Monthly Magazine*, August 1877.

From the author's collection

looking "dim and distant blue." Each time he stood on one mountaintop, he saw others that intrigued him. And he and Hoar still had more traveling to do.

Two days later, the two men had driven the horse and carriage as close to Mount Washington as they could. From this point on, they would have to climb. They hired a local man named Wentworth to help carry their bags and to provide knowledgeable advice. But Thoreau couldn't wait. He got up early the next morning and climbed to the top of Mount Washington by himself. He was rewarded with a clear view from the summit. By the time Hoar and Wentworth caught up to him, misty clouds had moved in. Thoreau knew how lucky he had been, and he understood the dangers that could arise under these circumstances. "It is unwise for one to ramble over these mountains at any time, unless he is prepared to move with as much certainty as if he were solving a geometrical problem," he said. "A cloud may at any moment settle around him, and unless he has a compass and knows which way to go, he will be lost at once." In Tuckerman Ravine, the group was soon met by his Worcester friends, H. G. O. Blake and Theo Brown, who had had trouble finding them. The five men spent a cool and rainy night sleeping in a tent.

Thoreau had a great time with his companions, climbing mountains and collecting and identifying many native plants. The excursion was not without its challenges, however. Icy patches of snow could still be found in spots, even in July. At times he and Hoar accidentally lost one another temporarily. "If you take one side of a rock, and your companion another, it is enough to separate you sometimes for the rest of the ascent." And on one outing, Thoreau sprained his ankle. He evidently landed wrong when he jumped into or across a brook. The pain was enough to keep him sitting in camp for a full day. Gradually, he worked through the minor injury. He was able to join his friends in exploring Tuckerman Ravine, the gorge right next to the mountain. They also had a chance to climb Mount Lafayette (5,249 ft.) before heading home to Massachusetts. Overall, it was a successful trip.

When Thoreau later heard of a legal battle between two men who both claimed to own the land at Mount Washington's summit, he found the news distasteful. "I think that the top of Mt. Washington should not be private property," he said. "It should be left unappropriated for modesty and reverence's sake, or if only to suggest that earth has higher uses than we put her to." Soon afterward, both the cog railway and the new carriage road were completed. At least two hotels stood on the summit. It was now even easier for the average tourist to ride up, to look around, to stay a while, or to go right back down the slope.

Today Thoreau would probably be pleased to know that Mount Washington is now protected as a state park. So are the rest of the other larger mountains that he visited: Wachusett,

Monadnock, Greylock, and Katahdin. A few of them also border state or national forests. Three lie along the popular Appalachian Trail. Now that they are protected from lumber and farming industries, the mountains have many more trees, plants, and other wildlife living on them than they did when he visited them a century and a half ago—in addition to some of the same plants that he saw back then. They also have more people climbing and enjoying them.

Hill or mountain, small or tall, any part of the land that rose up from a plain became a magnet for Thoreau. He liked them for the inspiring sights they provided in the distance, for the interesting habitats they provided to the wildlife that lived on them, for the views that could be gained from their summits, and for the spiritual experiences he found in their heights. The life that existed down below looked quite different when seen from above. Up here, closer to the clouds, Thoreau felt even more connected to the natural world and to the larger universe. "I suppose that I feel the same awe when on their summits that many do on entering a church."

Today's Appalachian Trail

Some of the paths along the peaks and ranges that Thoreau climbed—through the White Mountains, and over Mount Greylock, Mount Washington, and Mount Katahdin—are now part of the Appalachian Trail. This route is more than 2,180 miles long, and it follows the ridges and valleys of the Appalachian Mountains through 14 states, from Maine to Georgia.

This trail did not exist in Thoreau's day. Another Harvard graduate came up with the idea for it, however. Benton MacKaye (1879–1975) was a trained forester and a regional planner who spent much of his life in Shirley, Massachusetts, just four towns west of Concord. In 1921, he proposed the creation of a series of camps linked by trails in the Appalachians, in order for people from the nearby cities to have places to go to enjoy nature and relax. The trail finally became a reality in 1937.

Today, thousands of local volunteers work to maintain it by trimming trees, building bridges, and repairing overnight shelters. Each year several million people walk along at least part of the Appalachian Trail. And each year, some "thru-hikers" complete the entire route in one continuous five- or six-month trek. They usually hike northward, starting at Springer Mountain in Georgia in the springtime and reaching Mount Katahdin in Maine by the fall. Katahdin is just as much a goal for hikers today as it was for Thoreau in the 1850s.

A number of other National Scenic Trails cross parts of the United States. Examples include the Pacific Crest Trail (in California, Oregon, and Washington), the Continental Divide Trail (in New Mexico, Colorado, Wyoming, Idaho, and Montana), and the North Country Trail (in North Dakota, Minnesota, Wisconsin, Michigan, Ohio, Pennsylvania, and New York). Does your state have its own trail system? Are any of the national trails located close to your home? Have you hiked along them?

Shells on a Cape Cod beach, photo by
Herbert W. Gleason.

The Thoreau Institute at Walden Woods

5

GOING FARTHER AFIELD

Despite his reputation as a hermit, Thoreau got around quite a bit. Sometimes he traveled to give public lectures. Most often this meant taking the train to other towns and cities in Massachusetts. He delivered more than 70 readings in his lifetime, speaking in halls as far south and west as Philadelphia, Pennsylvania, and as far north and east as Portland, Maine. He talked about his years at Walden Pond, about his night spent in the Middlesex County jail, or about his visits to Maine, Cape Cod, or Quebec. He tried out his material on his listening audiences first before he wrote the final drafts of his essays.

Surveying work also led him into neighboring towns. He even took on the job of outlining a large property in Perth Amboy, New Jersey, in 1856. Being outside and walking around a piece of land gave him a chance to study the plants and animals of the area, too. Thoreau made additional trips to specific sites to study old trees, to understand tree succession, or to figure out the methods plants used to distribute their seeds. These were projects that he assigned to himself.

Thoreau wrote in *Walden*, "I have travelled a good deal in Concord." This statement can be misleading. Yes, he was familiar with nearly every inch of his hometown landscape. But he also spent time in 15 northern states and 2 present-day Canadian provinces. He traveled as deliberately as he lived. He always had a reason for going somewhere. He never took what we would consider today to be a vacation or a getaway to do absolutely nothing. He was always observing and taking notes.

Worcester (1849–1861)

After railroad lines were laid in the early 1840s, Thoreau used them often. One of his favorite destinations was the city of Worcester, Massachusetts, which was a 43-mile train ride away. Thoreau had friends here, and he visited them at least a dozen times. He gave nine lectures in Worcester (pronounced "WUSS-ter"). Even the two-hour trip was beneficial, because Thoreau could "botanize" from the train windows along the way. He could watch for changes in the familiar landscape and could notice what flowers were blooming, what leaves were turning colors, or

even which way the snow was blowing. He took notes on what he saw.

Worcester had about 20,000 residents during Thoreau's lifetime, making it 10 times bigger than Concord. His main contact here was teacher Harrison Gray Otis Blake. Blake and his friend Theo Brown lived in homes a few blocks away from the city's main street. These men were first fans of Thoreau's writing, and they grew to become some of his closest friends.

Blake was a year younger than Thoreau. He too was a Harvard graduate, but he began his career as a minister before he switched to teaching. He met Ralph Waldo Emerson, exchanged letters with him, and was invited to the Emerson home in Concord for intellectual parlor discussions. Blake and Thoreau ran into one another there once.

In 1848, Blake read an essay that Thoreau had published in the *Dial*. He was so impressed that he felt the need to write the author a letter. The two men began a correspondence and a friendship that lasted 14 years. They enjoyed holding philosophical conversations on paper and in person.

Blake and Brown were probably responsible for making arrangements for Thoreau to lecture in Worcester. They all shared interests in philosophy and nature. They held literary discussions with friends in their living rooms. Together they explored the shoreline of nearby Lake Quinsigamond and studied the exhibits of some of the city's museums. The Worcester men could

Main Street, Worcester, Massachusetts, from John Warner Barber's *Historical Collections*, 1841.

From the author's collection

always offer Henry a place to stay when he was in town.

When it came time to return the favor, Thoreau sent Blake an invitation in the form of a pun: "Come & be Concord, as I have been Worcestered." Blake and Brown visited Thoreau and sometimes chose to take a few days to walk from Worcester instead of taking the train. Blake also accompanied Thoreau on trips to Mount Wachusett and Mount Monadnock. He was Thoreau's best friend away from Concord.

Worcester, like Concord, is very different today. The city is now home to more than 181,000 residents. It is the second largest city in New England, behind Boston and before Providence, Rhode Island. Quite a number of downtown buildings that Thoreau saw and visited are still standing today. Mechanics Hall, where he spoke passionately about abolitionist John Brown in 1859, still hosts concerts and events. The podium that Thoreau lectured from is still used by speakers and entertainers.

Cape Cod

Henry visited the Maine wilderness three times (including his climb of Katahdin) and the beaches of Cape Cod four times. The cape is a narrow, sandy arm of land that extends from mainland Massachusetts into the Atlantic Ocean. The easiest way for Thoreau to get there was to take a steamer from Boston and cross Cape Cod Bay to reach Provincetown, the tiny settlement at

Henry's Worcester Friends

Harrison Gray Otis Blake (1818–1898) was a Harvard graduate and a teacher at a private girls' school. He admired Emerson first, of all of the transcendentalists, after the man spoke at Harvard's graduation ceremony in 1838. Blake spent only one year working as a minister in New Hampshire before taking the teaching job in Worcester. He began corresponding with Thoreau in 1848. They sent dozens of letters to each other over the years, until Thoreau's death in 1862. Blake would gather friends around and read Henry's letters aloud, so that the group could discuss them. Blake inherited Thoreau's journals in 1876.

Theophilus "Theo" Brown (1811–1879) was a tailor who was often described as "the wit of Worcester." He accompanied Blake on trips to Concord and on tours around Worcester with Henry. He was an accomplished letter writer, too. But Thoreau corresponded only with Blake.

Other friends and members of this Worcester literary group were:

Thomas Wentworth Higginson (1823–1911) was a writer and minister. Today he is best known as one of John Brown's "Secret Six" supporters and as the person who befriended Emily Dickinson and published her first anthology of poetry. He served as the pastor of the Free Church on Front Street. Higginson volunteered for duty during the Civil War and led the country's first all-black infantry regiment, the First South Carolina Volunteers.

Henry Harmon Chamberlin (1813–1899) was a local self-published poet.

Reverend Horace James (1818–1875) was the pastor of the Old South Church on the Worcester Common. He collected reptiles and amphibians, and Thoreau visited his display rooms.

David Atwood Wasson (1822–1887) was a transcendentalist minister and writer.

Edward Everett Hale (1822–1909) was a Unitarian minister and writer.

Dr. Seth Rogers (1823–1893) was a general physician who used "hydrology," the water cure. He served as a surgeon for Thomas Wentworth Higginson's regiment during the Civil War.

Martha H. (LeBaron) Goddard (1829–1888) was a writer and civil rights activist.

the very end of the peninsula. Ellery Channing accompanied Thoreau on two of these trips.

Thoreau noticed that the beach habitat was quite different from the farms and the forests that he knew in Concord. First of all, there were no trees here, since the residents had cut them all down to use for wood. The cape had another sort of wildness to it, too. "It is a wild, rank place, and there is no flattery in it," he wrote. He found the sandy shoreline "strewn with crabs, horse-shoes, and razor-clams, and whatever the sea casts up." He eagerly picked up some of these natural treasures, and even found an old French coin on the beach.

But shellfish and pebbles weren't the only things that washed up on shore. In July 1855, Thoreau witnessed fishermen driving hundreds of small pilot whales (which he called "black-fish") toward the beach in order to harvest them. The torn carcasses were left behind after the men had cut away and taken the blubber and the meat. "Walking on the beach was out of the question on account of the stench," he wrote.

Henry Thoreau's handmade box for geological specimens.
Concord Museum,
www.concordmuseum.org

Debris from shipwrecks also landed on shore. The waters around the cape were rocky and sandy and could prove dangerous for ship captains to navigate. In 1849, Thoreau saw this firsthand after

the *St. John,* a ship carrying Irish immigrants, wrecked near Cohasset. Only 20 passengers survived; 99 had died. Two days later, people were still picking through the remains of the ship and were working to identify the bodies. Thoreau was overwhelmed in his own way by the tragedy. "If I had found one body cast upon the beach in some lonely place, it would have affected me more," he thought. To see so many ship timbers and personal possessions piled high made the great loss seem unreal and almost easier to deal with.

Those sights aside, Thoreau felt a sense of freedom while walking these beaches. What was it like to be on this shore, looking out at the Atlantic Ocean, knowing that you were at the most eastern edge of the country? "A man may stand there and put all America behind him," he said. "The time must come when this coast will be a place of resort for those New-Englanders who really wish to visit the sea-side. At present it is wholly unknown to the fashionable world, and probably it will never be agreeable to them."

He predicted the cape's future fairly accurately. It is now a popular area for artists and vacationers alike. Its land is also protected in part by the Cape Cod National Seashore. Some would say that it has indeed become "fashionable" to go there.

Quebec

In September 1850, Henry and Ellery Channing made a weeklong trip north to Quebec, in what

Study Grains of Sand

"See a scum on the smooth surface of the lake 3 or 4 feet from shore—The color of the sand of the shore—like pollen & lint—which I took it to be. Taking some up in my hand, I was surprised to find it the sand of the shore—sometimes pretty large grains 1/10 inch diameter—but most 1/20 or less; some dark brown, some white or yellowish—some minute but perfectly regular oval pebbles of white quartz. I suppose that the water rises [and] gently lifts up a layer of sand where it is slightly cemented by some glutinous matter, for I felt a slight stickiness in my hand after the (gravel or) sand was shaken off." Henry wrote these field notes when he explored the edge of Lake Calhoun in Minnesota in the summer of 1861.

You can look closely at sand, too. The single grains are actually tiny bits of rocks that have been worn down by the actions of wind and water over time.

WHAT YOU NEED

- A heaping spoonful of dry sand
- Magnifying glass
- Toothpick
- Paper plate
- Tweezers (optional)
- Glass jar (optional)
- Label (optional)

Get a small amount of sand from a natural source: a beach, a riverbed, a quarry, or a patch of desert. If you don't have a place like this near you, ask someone who travels to bring some back to you. (Do not purchase sand in a store unless it is absolutely necessary.) Make sure it is dry. If it sticks together in a clump, then spread it out and let it dry for a day.

Drop the spoonful of sand in the middle of the paper plate. Take a moment to write about the sand in your journal. What color do you think it is? White? Tan? Brown? Gray? Black? Touch it. Smell it. Record your findings.

Look at it through the magnifying glass. Using the toothpick or a pair of tweezers, push the sand around. Separate the individual grains by color. There will probably be at least three major colors. The white or clear grains are likely to be quartz. Tan grains will be from sedimentary rocks, like sandstone. Darker grains may come from metamorphic or igneous rocks. The mixture will depend upon where the sand came from and what rocks crumbled to make it.

Which color pile has the most grains? Does this surprise you? Record your findings. You may want to do more research or ask a science teacher for help in identifying the kinds of rocks represented in your sand sample. Afterward, you can keep your sand in a clear glass jar, along with any shells and rocks you may have gathered at the same place. Attach a label marked with where and when you found them.

Robert DePaolo

Build a Rock Collection Box

"We eagerly filled our pockets with the smooth round pebbles which in some places, even here, were thinly sprinkled over the sand, together with flat circular shells . . . but, as we had read, when they were dry they had lost their beauty, and at each sitting we emptied our pockets again of the least remarkable, until our collection was well culled." Here on Cape Cod, Henry picked up the rocks he liked, then decided in the end which ones were good enough to save. Where could he keep them? In a "box for geological specimens" which he built for himself out of wood.

You can make a similar box out of cardboard in order to protect and organize your own rock collection.

WHAT YOU NEED

- Empty shoe box or another smallish cardboard box
- Extra cardboard that is at least the same size as the box
- Scissors
- Labels or small paper strips
- Ruler

Measure the length and width of the box. Cut one piece of cardboard to match the length of the box. Cut three pieces to match its width.

Slide the long piece into the box, standing it up in the middle. It should divide the space into two long and equal parts. You may have to trim the piece along one end. Make sure it fits snugly.

Remove that piece from the box. Now test the three smaller pieces so that they stand and fit in the other direction. Trim them as necessary. Remove them from the box.

Measuring the long piece lengthwise, draw a line at the halfway point. Draw a line at each of the halfway points of these halves. You should have made three marks that divide the piece into quarters. At each mark, cut the cardboard about halfway across the width of the piece.

On each one of the short pieces, mark the halfway point. At each mark, cut the cardboard about halfway across the width of each piece. Now each of the four cardboard pieces should have "teeth."

Put the long piece into the box with the cuts facing up. Slide the smaller pieces onto it with their cuts facing down. The resulting grid should divide the box into eight spaces for rocks or other collectibles.

If tissue paper came with the box, you may want to keep it at the bottom in order to give a bit of added protection to your samples. Place a rock in each compartment and label it with its name and where and when you found it.

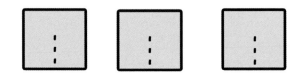

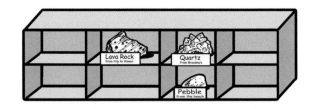

was then called the United Province of Canada. They took a series of trains to Burlington, Vermont; crossed Lake Champlain by steamer; and then used a combination of trains and watercraft to reach Montreal. They sailed down the St. Lawrence River to the area around Quebec City. Why did they go? Perhaps just due to curiosity about the place. "I wished only to be set down in Canada, and take one honest walk there as I might in Concord woods of an afternoon," Thoreau said. Off they went.

In Montreal, they toured the Notre Dame Basilica, which had been built in 1829. The Roman Catholic cathedral was unlike any church Thoreau had ever seen. "It was a great cave in the midst of a city," he said. "Such a cave at hand, which you can enter any day, is worth a thousand of our churches which are open only Sundays, —hardly enough for an airing. . . . I think that I might go to church myself sometimes some Monday, if I lived in a city where there was such a one to go to. In Concord, to be sure, we do not need such. Our forests are such a church, far grander and more sacred." Although he thought the stone structures of Quebec were interesting too, he wasn't fond of the city walls and their gates. Or at least not with the soldiers who still kept guard at them.

The two friends traveled by boat along the St. Lawrence River and stopped to explore the Montmorency Falls and the waterfalls at Canyon Sainte-Anne. They saw so many waterfalls along the steep banks of the river's tributaries that they almost got tired of seeing them. "Falls there are a drug; and we became quite dissipated in respect to them," he said. "We had drank too much of them."

What they weren't used to was the challenge of communicating with the people who lived in the small towns of this countryside. "We soon found that the inhabitants were exclusively French Canadian, and nobody spoke English at all, any more than in France; that, in fact, we were in a foreign country, where the inhabitants uttered not one familiar sound to us. Then we tried by turns to talk French with them, in which we succeeded sometimes pretty well, but for the most part, pretty ill." The men got by well enough to find places to stay each night. Soon enough, they turned around and headed back to Vermont and Massachusetts.

Four years after Thoreau's death, his descriptions about this trip appeared in the book *A Yankee in Canada, with Anti-Slavery and Reform Papers.* Just five chapters covered the whole adventure. The rest of the book contained ten of his essays on social justice, like "Civil Disobedience" and "Slavery in Massachusetts."

In these pages, Thoreau wasn't entirely complimentary about the land or the people of Canada, however. He thought everything seemed older there, as if it dated from the Middle Ages. Residents seemed to be stuck between the laws of the government and the demands of the church. He believed the British influence was too obvious and overwhelming. "In Canada you are reminded

Henry Thoreau, as drawn by friend Daniel Ricketson.
The Thoreau Institute at Walden Woods

H. D. Thoreau as he presented himself at the door of Brooklawn Dec 25 th 1854. age 37

What had impressed Thoreau most were the St. Lawrence River, the waterfalls, and some of the stone buildings. He even thought he might want to someday "make a longer excursion on foot through the wilder parts of Canada." (He didn't get this chance.) In the end, he summed up his experience to his readers by saying, "What I got by going to Canada was a cold."

On the Way to Brattleboro

One of Thoreau's smaller scientific excursions began with an unexpected diversion.

In the fall of 1856, he planned a trip to Brattleboro, Vermont, where he intended to spend a few days botanizing along the Connecticut River. He boarded the train in Concord on September 5 and headed west. When he reached the city of Fitchburg, he expected to continue his ride with the Vermont & Massachusetts Railroad. But each line was independently owned and operated, and they didn't always make direct connections.

Thoreau wrote in his journal: "Found on reaching Fitchburg that there was an interval of three and a half hours between this and the Brattleboro train, and so walked on, on the track, with shouldered valise." Was Thoreau going to sit around and wait for the next train to come? No. Why shouldn't his plant study start immediately? He picked up his bag and walked the five miles from the Fitchburg station to the one in Westminster. Along the way, he got a good look at the various species of goldenrods and asters

of the government every day. It parades itself before you," he said. "You could see England's hands holding the Canadas, and I judged by the redness of her knuckles that she would soon have to let go." Canada later became a Dominion, a self-governing country with ties to the United Kingdom, in 1867.

that were blooming right next to the tracks. Three hours later the train caught up to him in Westminster, and Thoreau continued his trip to Vermont by rail.

If he had studied the train timetable exactly, Thoreau would have noticed the three and a half hour gap in the schedule. But if he had taken the later train from Concord, then he wouldn't have had the chance to walk among the flowers of fall on such a nice day. When situations didn't turn out quite the way he first expected, he adapted to them in his own style. In this case, he shouldered his valise—his bag—and walked to Westminster.

Journey West

For much of his life, Thoreau suffered from consumption (today called tuberculosis), a lung disease that affected many people in the 19th century. His symptoms worsened after he caught a cold in December 1860. Doctors didn't know then that consumption was contagious and that it was passed from one person to another. As a result, they often recommended that their patients travel to a different climate, believing that merely breathing better or clearer air would bring relief.

Thoreau decided to use his doctor's advice to make a long trip to the American Midwest. It was something that he had wanted to do for a long time. "Eastward I go only by force; but westward I go free," he said in his "Walking" lecture. His companion on this trip was 17-year-old Horace Mann Jr., son of the famous educator

Horace Mann. Young Horace lived in Concord and studied plants and animals on his own. He brought specimens to Thoreau so they could examine and identify them together. Thoreau must have thought he would make an able traveling companion.

In May 1861, the two men took trains to cross Massachusetts, New York, Canada West (southern Ontario), Michigan, and Illinois. They stopped at Niagara Falls and explored the area for five days. When they reached the Mississippi River at present-day East Dubuque, they boarded the *Itasca*, a steamboat. It took them several days to sail upriver and reach St. Paul. They spent the next month exploring the plains and prairies of Minnesota. Mann had brought his shotgun, and he collected gophers, passenger pigeons, and other small animals. Thoreau had brought his plant press and his botanic manuals. He kept a field notebook and recorded as many observations and species found as he could.

He was especially mystified by a tree with white-and-pink flowers that he spotted while crossing Michigan and Illinois. From the train windows, he could see the blooms in the distance. But it wasn't until he was in Minnesota that he was able to take the time to track down similar trees. They turned out to be crab apples. This was not a native species in New England, and Thoreau had never seen one in person. Folks from Virginia and Kentucky who had settled in Minnesota had brought the trees with them to plant in their new homes. Thoreau was lucky

Collect and Swap Seeds

"Though I do not believe a plant will spring up where no seed has been, I have great faith in a seed, —a, to me, mysterious origin for it. Convince me that you have a seed there, and I am prepared to expect wonders." Henry spoke these words at a meeting of local farmers in Concord in September 1860. He told of a time when he planted a few squash seeds, and his garden grew five large yellow squashes that weighed a total of 310 pounds. *"A little mysterious hoeing and manuring was all the abracadabra presto-change that I used,"* he said. It started with seeds.

What do you do with the seeds that you find in the middle of an orange or in a piece of watermelon? Do you throw them away? Why not try to plant them and grow more fruit yourself? You can collect seeds that will grow into all kinds of plants in your yard or that will supply fruits and vegetables for the dinner table. Once you have gathered them, you can share and swap your seeds with friends and relatives.

WHAT YOU NEED

- Small clear containers to hold seeds (glass jars with lids, clear plastic bags that seal, etc.)
- Labels and pen

If you have conducted a plant inventory (page 11) or are tending a garden (pages 26–27), then you already know what kinds of plants you have. If you are a beginner, then you may have to first figure out what plants are available in your area. Then you can experiment with them. Nature is diverse, and all seeds are different. Here are some guidelines:

1. Stay local. Collect seeds only from plants that are suited for growing in your region.

2. Know their names. If you buy the original fruit, vegetable, or plant from a farmer's market, grocery store, or nursery, then be sure to write down the variety's name from the posted sign or label.

3. Once you collect them, keep the seeds in different containers and mark them accurately.

4. Plant some seeds to see what happens. This may take some time, perhaps a whole growing season. And the plants that come up may not be exactly the same as the kinds you got the seeds from. If the seeds don't sprout within a week or two, you may have to do some research to learn the best methods for harvesting, processing, and storing that particular kind of seed. You may have to ask a local gardener for help.

5. Collect more seeds from the plants you grow! Keep the cycle going, and you can share more seeds with others.

Here are some of the easiest seeds to collect, plant, and swap:

Edibles	Native Plants
Beans	Oaks (acorn)
Peas	Maples (wings)
Pumpkins	Milkweed (seeds)
Sunflowers	
Tomatoes	
Watermelons	

For more information, check out the websites of the International Seed Saving Institute (www.seedsave.org) and the Seed Savers Exchange (www.seedsavers.org). You can also consult the resources of the community project based in Thoreau's hometown, the Concord Seed Lending Library (www.concordseedlendinglibrary.org).

Rob DePaolo

enough to find one and to cut off a small sprig for his herbarium, his plant collection.

In June, Henry and Horace joined a steamboat excursion heading up the Minnesota River to see the Dakota Indians at the Lower Sioux Agency in Redwood. This trip had been designed by

The Thoreau collection at the Concord Museum includes Dakota buckskins from Minnesota.
Lynn Sugarman

government officials in order to make the annual treaty payments to the natives. More than one hundred additional people went along to see the event. Even though the payment process itself was delayed, the travelers did have a chance to witness an intercultural meeting, a dance accompanied by native flutes and drums, and an ox roast.

Thoreau had a fondness for anything related to American Indians, and he must have been captivated by the scene. The members of the Dakota tribes were different from the few natives he had met back east in Massachusetts and in Maine. "A regular council was held with the Indians, who had come in on their ponies," he wrote. "Speeches were made on both sides thro' an interpreter, quite in the described mode; the Indians, as usual, having the advantage in point of truth and earnestness, and therefore of eloquence. . . . They were quite dissatisfied with the white man's treatment of them & probably have reason to be so." Even as a visitor, he could sense the tensions between the two sides.

Somehow Thoreau picked up three pieces of decorated buckskin clothing to take home with him. They could remind him of the very real American Indians he had seen and met out west.

Henry and Horace's Midwestern adventure was cut short by news of the Northern troop losses in the Civil War battle at Big Bethel,

Virginia. Since no one knew where the fighting would lead next, the two men returned home along a more northern route. They sailed across Lake Michigan and Lake Huron by steamboat, spending a few days on Mackinac Island in the process. They crossed Canada and northern New York to get back to New England. Although neither man ever had a chance to write about the experience, they both may have considered the trip a scientific success. They had seen some fascinating places and had met some interesting people. They had both gathered new species for their own natural history collections.

Home Sweet Home

Even though Thoreau was able to visit sites in the northern United States and southeastern Canada during his lifetime, he thought that nothing he had seen could compare to what he had back in Concord. "Here is a more interesting horizon, more variety and richness," he wrote in September 1858. He was incredibly devoted to his hometown. Traveling—and reading travel narratives written by others—made for nice and occasional outings. But he never wanted to live anywhere else.

Thoreau Farm—Birthplace of
Henry David Thoreau.
Rob DePaolo

6

AN ENDURING LEGACY

When Henry came home from Minnesota in July 1861, he knew his consumption was not cured. His friends and family members understood this, too. As his health continued to decline, Sophia helped her brother with the work they had started before he had left for the Midwest: preparing some of his favorite essays for publication.

Henry also traveled one last time to New Bedford, Massachusetts, to visit his friend Daniel Ricketson. There he sat stoically for an ambrotype picture to be taken, which was a process that placed a wet and shaded image of his face onto a glass plate. Ricketson thought it was "one of the most successful likenesses we ever saw." Thoreau's sister Sophia agreed: "I discover a slight shade about the eyes expressive of weariness, but a stranger might not observe it." His family and friends knew all too well that Thoreau was weary, ill, and growing weaker.

The months dragged in Concord. Thoreau abandoned his journal, and he rarely went outside. Instead, his closest friends and acquaintances visited him. Bronson Alcott, Ralph Waldo Emerson, and Ellery Channing stopped by to see Thoreau on a regular basis. H. G. O. Blake and Theo Brown traveled from Worcester. Thoreau was weak but calm. His one-time jailer, Sam Staples, dropped in and said that he "never saw a man dying with so much pleasure and peace." Not even illness could entirely dampen Thoreau's quick mind and sense of humor. One of his aunts asked him if he had made his peace with God. He replied, "I did not know we had ever quarreled."

Reports vary about Thoreau's final words. Ellery Channing claimed that Thoreau's recent work on his Maine essays resulted in him saying simply "moose" and "Indians." But Channing was not at his friend's side at the very end. Henry's

mother, sister, and Aunt Louisa were. Sophia chose to read aloud her brother's own words to him, from *A Week on the Concord and Merrimack Rivers*. Recalling that wonderful trip with their brother John, Henry whispered before his last breath, "Now comes good sailing."

Henry David Thoreau died at home in their living room on the morning of May 6, 1862. He was 44 years old.

The entire town of Concord mourned the loss. Children were excused early from school to attend the funeral. The bell of First Parish Church was rung 44 times. During the service, the choir sang a special hymn written by Ellery Channing. Bronson Alcott read portions of Thoreau's writings. Ralph Waldo Emerson delivered the eulogy. Thoreau had been a teacher, a writer, a lecturer, a surveyor, a pencil maker, an activist, a natural philosopher, and an amateur yet detail-oriented scientist. Emerson was disappointed that his friend had not become famous or well known outside of Concord. "No truer American existed than Thoreau," he said. "The country knows not yet, or in the least part, how great a son it has lost."

First Fans: Family and Friends

The diligence of Thoreau's closest fans paid off. After his death, *Atlantic Monthly* printed seven of Thoreau's pieces, including "Walking," "Wild Apples," and "Life Without Principle." Four new

(*right*) The Thoreau-Alcott or "Yellow" House, Henry's last residence.
Rob DePaolo

(*below*) Henry Thoreau in August 1861.
Concord Free Public Library

books of essays were published over the next four years: *Excursions* (1863), *The Maine Woods* (1864), *Cape Cod* (1864), and *A Yankee in Canada, with Anti-Slavery and Reform Papers* (1866). Emerson put together a volume of Thoreau's letters in 1865. The book *Walden* itself was also republished in 1862. The first edition had sold out in Thoreau's last years. It has not been out of print since.

Sophia Thoreau did as much to promote her brother's legacy as she could. When she died in 1876, Henry's notebooks and journals passed on to H. G. O. Blake of Worcester. Blake may not have known what to do what them at first. He eventually found a public audience at the Concord School of Philosophy. This series of adult education classes was hosted by Bronson Alcott. They were held during the summers of 1879–1888, either in Alcott's old home, called the Orchard House, or in the newly built wooden School of Philosophy building just across the lawn. People came from all over the Northeast and New England to attend.

Blake read aloud excerpts from Thoreau's journal for the first time here on August 6, 1879. He found eager listeners. Eliza Elvira Kenyon, principal of the Plainfield Seminary for girls in New Jersey, was in the room and was moved by the experience. "Every passage read by Mr. Blake deserved to be written in Light," she wrote in her own journal. Blake and Frank Sanborn read more selections during the next six years of the school sessions. Blake was encouraged to assemble passages from Thoreau's journal into four seasonal

The Concord School of Philosophy building today.
Rob DePaolo

volumes: *Early Spring in Massachusetts* (1881), *Summer* (1884), *Winter* (1888), and *Autumn* (1892). Now more of Thoreau's words were available for anyone to read.

People could also learn more about Thoreau's life from a few friends who had witnessed it firsthand. Ellery Channing wrote the first biography, titled *Thoreau: The Poet-Naturalist*, which

Henry David Thoreau's grave.
Rob DePaolo

was published in 1873. Frank Sanborn wrote and edited several related books, including the biography *Henry D. Thoreau* (1882) and *The First and Last Journeys of Thoreau* (1905). Unfortunately, many of his other friends had passed away. Nathaniel Hawthorne died in 1864; Ralph Waldo Emerson, in 1882; and both Bronson and Louisa Alcott, in 1888. All were buried in Sleepy Hollow Cemetery in a section referred to as Authors Ridge.

In the early 1870s, Thoreau's grave was moved up to Authors Ridge. The Thoreau plot had originally been set next to the Dunbars, the relatives of Henry's mother, Cynthia. Members of both families were buried at the bottom edge of the New Burying Ground along Bedford Street,

down the road from Sleepy Hollow. But someone—maybe Sophia Thoreau—decided that the Thoreaus deserved to be buried with the more famous Concordians. Once the graves were moved, the whole family was just a few steps away from the final resting places of the Hawthornes and the Alcotts. The large Emerson plot was located down a nearby path.

This position made it easier for out-of-town pilgrims to come and pay their respects to the entire group of transcendentalists at once. Many visitors also walked to Walden Pond, to see where Thoreau's house had once stood. The building itself was long gone. It had first been hauled away and used for storing grain at a local farm. Years later it was taken apart, and the roof was placed on a barn for pigs. The rest of the wood was put to use elsewhere. New Englanders regularly moved and reused houses and parts of buildings as they saw fit, placing the structures where they would work best. The Walden house disappeared into the rest of the Concord landscape.

The shoreline had changed since Thoreau's time there, too. In 1866, an amusement park called "Lake Walden" was created at Ice Fort Cove, next to the railroad tracks at the western edge of the pond. Lake Walden included concession stands, a playground, a bath house, a dance hall with live music, sports fields, and a race track on a nearby hill. Trains stopped there and deposited Bostonians and other visitors to the pond on a regular basis. People could swim at the beach, take boat rides, or enjoy walking around the woods. Summer days could now become quite noisy at Walden. Not everyone appreciated Thoreau's connection to this place or saw it as a special one.

In June 1872, Mary Newbury Adams of Iowa visited Walden with Bronson Alcott during a Unitarian church picnic. Bronson showed her where Thoreau's small house had once stood. Mary placed a stone on the spot, beginning the tradition of a cairn. Folks began adding stones to it.

Famous people started to come to Concord to pay tribute to Thoreau and his friends, too. In September 1881, New York poet Walt Whitman spent several days in Concord. He visited with the Emersons, the Sanborns, and the Alcotts, touring the town and seeing the Old Manse and the rebuilt North Bridge. He rode by horse up the hill to Sleepy Hollow Cemetery, then climbed the steep slope to Authors Ridge. On the path between Thoreau's grave and Nathaniel Hawthorne's, Whitman "stood a long while and ponder'd," he later wrote in *Specimen Days*. Then he rode "to Walden pond, that beautifully embower'd sheet of water, and spent over an hour there. On the spot in the woods where Thoreau had his solitary house is now quite a cairn of stones, to mark the place; I too carried one and deposited on the heap."

California naturalist and writer John Muir visited in the summer of 1893. He loved mountains too, but he preferred exploring the ones on the West Coast and in Alaska. Like Thoreau, he thought that some areas should be preserved for the public to enjoy. Yosemite National Park was named by Congress as one of the first wilderness parks in the United States in 1890, thanks to Muir's efforts. And when the Sierra Club formed as a hiking and advocacy group in 1892, Muir became its first president.

By the time of Muir's visit to Concord, the Emersons and Alcotts were gone. Muir and his friend Robert Underwood Johnson put flowers on Thoreau's grave and on Ralph Waldo Emerson's, too. Muir had never met Thoreau but he had met Emerson and had corresponded with him. "I did not imagine I would be so moved at sight of the resting-places of these grand men as I found I was," he wrote. "I think it is the most beautiful graveyard I ever saw."

Muir and Johnson walked to Walden Pond, probably following one of the paths that Thoreau and Emerson had used themselves years earlier. Muir thought the place was beautiful. "No wonder Thoreau lived here two years," he wrote. "I could have enjoyed living here two hundred years or two thousand. It is only about one and a half or two miles from Concord, a mere saunter, and how people should regard Thoreau as a hermit on account of his little delightful stay here I cannot guess."

A Second Wave

Now new biographies were written by people who hadn't even known Thoreau during his lifetime. They learned about him only by reading

The Cairn at Walden

Mary Newbury Adams and her husband, Austin, met Bronson Alcott when he stopped in Dubuque, Iowa, on his lecture tour in 1870. In June 1872, Mary traveled to Concord to visit with the Alcotts in return. She and Bronson attended a Unitarian picnic at the new amusement park at Walden Pond. It had been 25 years since Henry had lived there. His small wooden house was long gone. But Bronson knew where it had stood, and he led the picnickers to the spot. Mary Adams decided to commemorate the site by starting a cairn, a Gaelic tradition of using natural materials as a landmark. Bronson wrote:

> Mrs. Adams suggests that visitors to Walden shall bring a small stone for Thoreau's monument and begins the pile by laying stones on the site of his hermitage, which I point out to her. The tribute thus rendered to our friend may, as the years pass, become a pile to his memory. The rude stones were a monument more fitting than the costliest carving of the artist. Henry's fame is sure to brighten with years, and this spot visited by admiring readers of his works.

The pile soon took on a life of its own. It got larger and larger, decade after decade. In 1945, some members of the Thoreau Society stood before it and wondered: *Were the rocks really piled exactly where Henry's house had been?*

Roland Wells Robbins launched an impromptu archaeological dig to determine the exact position of Thoreau's Walden house. By October 1945, he had found the chimney foundation and was able to plot the former footprint of the structure. The cairn was in the right place after

all. In fact, it had to be moved slightly for granite house markers to be installed.

In 1975, all of the rocks and stones were temporarily taken away by the Commonwealth of Massachusetts, which managed the property as Walden Pond State Reservation. The authorities had called the cairn "unsightly." After much protest, the rocks were brought back in 1978.

Today visitors still add to the memorial cairn at Walden Pond. They often bring stones from home. Some are inscribed or etched with names and dates.

The cairn today.
Rob DePaolo

Walden and his other books. Scottish author Alexander Hay Japp (1837–1905) wrote *Thoreau: His Life and Aims, A Study,* under the pseudonym H. A. Page, in 1877. Japp soon became friends with another Scottish writer and novelist, Robert Louis Stevenson (1850–1894). After the two men realized that they were both interested in Thoreau's life and writings, Stevenson published his own biography, *Henry David Thoreau: His Character and Opinions,* in 1880.

At the end of the 19th century, one of Thoreau's biggest fans lived in Ann Arbor, Michigan. Dr. Samuel Arthur Jones (1834–1912) was a homeopathic physician who served as the dean of the University of Michigan's Homeopathic Medical College. When he began to read the writings of Scottish philosopher and writer Thomas Carlyle, his study soon led him to the American transcendentalists and to Thoreau. Suddenly Dr. Jones wanted to learn everything and to read everything about him. He began to correspond with some of the remaining people in Massachusetts who had known his new idol: H. G. O. Blake, Daniel Ricketson, Frank Sanborn, Edward Emerson, and Alfred Winslow Hosmer. Dr. Jones wrote essays and delivered lectures about Thoreau. He made his own pilgrimage to Concord in August 1890.

Dr. Jones and his group also exchanged letters with Henry S. Salt (1851–1939), an English writer and reformer who was an avid vegetarian and an advocate of animal rights. These positions were not overwhelmingly popular at the time.

Out of this correspondence back and forth across the Atlantic Ocean grew Salt's biography, *Life of Henry David Thoreau,* in 1890. A second edition of the book was published to correct some errors in 1896. It is thought to be the best early biography, since it included researched information and details provided by Thoreau's friends and townsmen.

Because of his own interest in vegetarianism, Mohandas Gandhi of India had a chance to meet Henry Salt in England in the early part of the 20th century. The English reformer and the future Indian leader became friends. Gandhi had already read "Civil Disobedience" and was impressed. His desire to learn more about Thoreau led him to read Salt's biography. Gandhi would later count Thoreau as being one of his influences in dealing with his own national challenges. Thoreau's circle of influence was widening well beyond the East Coast of the United States. It reached around the world.

Not everyone who wrote about Thoreau was supportive, however. Some writers accused him of imitating his friend Emerson too much. Back in 1848, James Russell Lowell had written in his poem "A Fable for Critics" that to see Thoreau was "rare sport, Tread in Emerson's tracks with legs painfully short." In 1865, in an essay called "Thoreau," Lowell wrote: "He only saw the things he looked for, and was less poet than naturalist. . . . He discovered nothing. He thought everything a discovery of his own, from moonlight to the planting of acorns and nuts by squirrels. This is a defect in his character, but one of his chief charms as a writer." Although Lowell thought that someone wanting to find a connection with Nature had "a mark of disease," he did admit that he admired Thoreau's writing style. His sentences were "as perfect as anything in the language, and [his] thoughts as clearly crystallized; his metaphors and images are always fresh from the soil."

Robert Louis Stevenson was also painfully honest when he described his impression of Thoreau: "In one word, Thoreau was a skulker." But Stevenson later admitted that he admired the man for spending the night in jail to oppose "the misdeeds" of his country.

Other readers and writers were more favorably influenced. When he was a young boy, Irish poet William Butler Yeats (1865–1939) listened to his father read passages from *Walden* aloud. Yeats was inspired by the words and imagined having a special place of his own, just like Thoreau had at Walden. He knew of the perfect spot. In 1890, he published a poem about this very real island in Ireland, called "The Lake Isle of Innisfree," which begins with this verse:

> *I will arise and go now, and go to*
> *Innisfree,*
> *And a small cabin build there, of clay*
> *and wattles made:*
> *Nine bean rows will I have there, a hive*
> *for the honey-bee,*
> *And live alone in the bee-loud glade.*

Unfortunately, Yeats never had the opportunity to live there.

In Concord, the once-popular Lake Walden excursion and amusement park faded away. Fire destroyed the dance pavilion, a concession stand, and the railroad station in May 1900. Two years later, a few remaining buildings and a bridge burned down. By early 1904, everything was gone. Walden's amusement park era was over.

Ownership of Thoreau's journals and notebooks changed hands again when H. G. O. Blake died in 1898. This time the material went to E. Harlow Russell, who was then the president of Worcester Normal School (now Worcester State University). Russell wasn't the best caretaker of the books, however. Eventually he sold them to a private collector. They scattered to the homes of other wealthy buyers living around the country. But before this could happen, Russell made arrangements for the full set of Henry's writings to be published by Houghton, Mifflin and Company in 1906.

The Writings of Henry David Thoreau was 20 volumes long. Five volumes were reprints of Thoreau's individual published books. The sixth was a book of letters. The other 14 consisted of the text of most of Thoreau's journals. The set featured black-and-white photographs taken by Herbert W. Gleason, an outdoorsman, writer, and photographer who greatly admired Thoreau. Now people could read even more of Thoreau's words, and they could see some of the actual places where he had lived and walked.

The year 1917 marked the 100th anniversary of Henry Thoreau's birth. Although he had been gone for 55 years, his reputation continued to grow. New centenary biographies were written by Frank Sanborn (*The Life of Henry David Thoreau*) and Edward Emerson (*Henry Thoreau, As Remembered by a Young Friend*). Herbert W. Gleason compiled the earliest book to pair photographs with Thoreau's words. Called *Through the Year with Thoreau*, it included another variety of black-and-white photos of locations, plants, and scenery. The tradition of the illustrated Thoreau quote book was born.

His Circles Grow Even Wider

As the 20th century progressed, "Civil Disobedience" and parts of *Walden* began to appear in American literature textbooks. Students in high school and college classrooms learned more about Thoreau. They read his words and discussed them. One of these students was young Martin Luther King Jr. He read "Civil Disobedience" in an introductory philosophy class at Morehouse College in Atlanta in 1947. The idea of nonviolent resistance fascinated him. He soon turned to the writings of Mohandas Gandhi as well.

Several American educators began to exchange letters and to share their interest in Thoreau's life and work. The two main correspondents were Walter Harding, then a school principal in Northfield, Massachusetts, and Raymond Adams, an English professor at the University of North Carolina. They decided to meet in Concord on Saturday, July 12, 1941, and to invite others there to celebrate Thoreau's birthday. They were shocked when a large and enthusiastic crowd filled the hall to overflowing that day. Harding proposed that a group called The Thoreau Society be formed, and the motion was seconded. Adams was named the president, and Harding was voted in as secretary. The organization had to cancel its 1943 meeting because of the demands of World War II. Otherwise, it has been meeting in Concord ever since, during the week falling closest to Thoreau's birthday, July 12.

At first, the meetings consisted of talks and presentations on just one Saturday. Participants could visit Walden Pond and other sites around Concord on their own. But when the group celebrated its 50th anniversary in 1991, the celebration expanded to an Annual Gathering that lasted two weeks, with events held in the city of Worcester, too. Hundreds of people attended talks and took tours and hikes, following in Thoreau's footsteps. Today, the Thoreau Society's Annual Gathering lasts about four or five days and is open to group members and nonmembers alike. The group is proud "to stimulate interest in and foster education about Thoreau's life, works, legacy and his place in his world and in ours, challenging all to live a deliberate, considered life."

The year 1962 marked the 100th anniversary of Thoreau's death. Even more biographies and literary criticism books appeared. One of

The 1967 Henry David Thoreau stamp.

From the author's collection

the most important was a large illustrated book called *In Wildness Is the Preservation of the World*, published by the Sierra Club. American photographer Eliot Porter had paired his nature photographs with passages from Henry's writings. The title was a quote from Henry's essay "Walking." Every page was beautiful. This was also one of the first times such a volume was printed with stunning color photographs on quality paper. It set the standard for other coffee-table books to follow, including more by Porter, often on famous natural sites.

To honor the 150th anniversary of Thoreau's birth in 1967, the United States Post Office issued a special first-class stamp on July 12. It carried a portrait of Thoreau as interpreted and drawn by American sculptor and graphic artist Leonard Baskin. About 120 million of these stamps were printed, in sheets of 50. Now Thoreau traveled on envelopes farther around the country than he ever had in person. Whether he would have liked it or not, his face was seen by a large population.

America was in a culturally turbulent time in the 1960s and '70s. Some people looked at this stamp and saw a picture of a hippie wearing long hair and a beard. They thought he was a symbol of the counterculture, and something to be frowned upon. Others admired Thoreau and liked what they saw. They read *Walden* and his journals, and they took some of his ideas to heart.

This was an important time for Thoreau's growing reputation. In his books and essays, he had addressed these general themes:

- *The importance of nature and the environment*
- *The choice to live deliberately and simply*
- *The importance of human rights, civil rights, and individuality*
- *The role of the government in our lives*

Concerns about the environmental health of the planet grew so intense that the first Earth Day was held in 1970. Some individuals broke away from mainstream society and lived in communes, establishing their own lifestyles and rules. Some built their own tiny houses in the woods. The movements for civil rights and women's rights were in full swing, and so were protests against the United States' involvement in the war in Vietnam. Sit-ins were used as forms of nonviolent resistance and civil disobedience. Thoreau's words seemed to apply to every situation. They could be found printed on cards and posters. He may not have become famous in his own lifetime, but he sure was well known a century later.

Today the issues that Thoreau wrote about still number among our biggest challenges.

An Influential Man

What would Thoreau think of his fame? What would he think about people trying to mirror his beliefs or to live like him? "I would not have any one adopt *my* mode of living on any account,"

Simplify Your Stuff

"Simplicity, simplicity, simplicity! I say, let your affairs be as two or three, and not a hundred or a thousand," said Thoreau. "A man is rich in proportion to the number of things which he can afford to let alone." He lived simply and deliberately, especially when he was at his Walden house. Truthfully, this choice may have been easier for him. He didn't have as many options and distractions as we have today.

You can simplify what surrounds you. This task goes beyond just cleaning or straightening up a space.

WHAT YOU NEED

- 3 big boxes or plastic bins
- 3 pieces of paper
- Tape
- Marker

Place the boxes or bins on the floor in your space. Use the marker, paper, and tape to label each one:

> *Keep*
>
> *Give Away / Recycle*
>
> *Trash*

Now, go through every single thing in your space. Pick up the first item. Look at it and think about it. Do you really need it or use it? Is it broken? If it's a piece of clothing, does it still fit? Is it torn or in need of repair? Decide which category the item falls into. Should you keep it, give it away or recycle it, or throw it away entirely? Put it in that box. Continue with the next item.

If it seems too difficult to tackle a whole room this way, start with something smaller. Start with your backpack, your desk or dresser, or your closet. Empty it, consider each item, and place it into one of the category boxes. At the end, put the Keepers back where they should stay. Get ready to remove the contents of the other two bins.

Approach this task on your own first, and make your own decisions. Be sure to get an adult's opinions afterward, and ask for his or her permission before you redistribute your unnecessary stuff. You won't want to get rid of something that belongs to someone else or that will prove to be important to you later.

What will you do with the stuff in the Give Away / Recycle box? You can offer it to your friends and family members. You can have a yard sale. You can give the items to a local charity shop run by a nonprofit organization. Books can usually be donated to a public library for a future sales event.

Some of us are mess makers. Some of us are neat freaks. A lot of us fall between the two extremes. No matter what kind of person you are, you can benefit from this activity. Can you simplify your stuff once a year? Times that may work best are at the beginning of January or at the end of summer, just before school starts. When you are finished, you should be surrounded only by stuff that serves your needs or that makes you happy.

Compile a Quote Book

"Many a man has dated a new era in his life from the reading of a book," said Thoreau. A number of individuals could make the same statement about Walden. More people have heard or read Thoreau's words without even having read any of his books, too. He may be one of the most quoted American authors. You can find his sayings on posters and greeting cards, both in print and online. Each year collections of quotations from his writings are published. They often include beautiful photographs that match the spirit of his words.

You can compile your own book of favorite quotations, with or without illustrations. And the words don't all have to come from Thoreau.

WHAT YOU NEED

- Fresh notebook, journal, or computer file
- Pen or pencil
- Colored pencils, crayons, or paints (optional)
- Camera (optional)

Start collecting sayings that you like. Begin by considering the texts of some of your favorite books or movies, or something that you've heard a friend or a family member say. The words should be meaningful to you. You should feel some kind of connection to them. Each quote should be rather short, consisting of only one or two sentences, if possible. Write down or type

Rob DePaolo

the words exactly, in the middle of a single page. Be sure to give credit! Put the name of the author after each quotation.

If you want to add illustrations, then get out your paints, crayons, pencils, or camera. You could find suitable pictures or photos online or in printed magazines or books. However, if you use someone else's images for a publication, then you have to get permission from the originator or owner to use them. (We did just that, in assembling the illustrations for this book.) Can you draw your own scenes? Can you take your own photographs? You will find the task more satisfying if you create the illustrations yourself.

Here is an example that goes with the photograph on the opposite page:

Heaven is under our feet, as well as over our heads. —Henry David Thoreau, *Walden*

Once you have at least 20 to 25 quotations (and their pictures, if you wish), you can compile them into book format. Title the first page of the book "My Favorite

Quotes," followed by your name. Alternate the pages of text and illustrations so that people can read the quote, then see the accompanying picture. Publishers often arrange them as double-page spreads. When you open this kind of book, the words appear on the left-hand page and the picture appears on the right. But in this case, you are the editor. You can decide how your book should best be put together.

Share your book with friends and relatives! You may be asked to produce more copies or to add to the selection of quotes you already have.

Boston University's Climate Change Study

It wasn't until the 21st century that Thoreau's detailed charts and records of phenology—nature's calendar and its recurring plant and animal life-cycle stages—were considered truly valuable by scientists. The main interest came from two men at Boston University, located less than 20 miles southeast of Concord. Abe Miller-Rushing was working on his doctoral degree in biology and needed a research topic. Professor Richard B. Primack was helping him find seasonal data from the past to compare with their recent observations. The men were excited to learn of Henry Thoreau's historical scientific data in 2003. They spent the next three years walking around Concord and comparing what they could find with what Thoreau had seen more than 150 years earlier. The results vary, plant by plant. But some flowers definitely bloom much earlier now than they did in Thoreau's day. The ice on Walden Pond melts earlier in most years, too.

The general public first heard of this research in an article called "Teaming up with Thoreau," published in *Smithsonian* in October 2007. Primack shared more of the story in his 2014 book, *Walden Warming: Climate Change Comes to Thoreau's Woods*. Both men now encourage people to take part in "citizen science:" to keep phenologies in their own neighborhoods, and to share the information with others.

In March 1853, Thoreau had received an application in the mail to become a member of the American Association for the Advancement of Science (AAAS). He turned down this opportunity, explaining that he "should not be able to attend the meetings," which were held in Washington, DC. But privately in his journal, he gave the real reason for his decision: he was afraid he wouldn't fit in. "I felt that it would be to make myself the laughing-stock of the scientific community to describe or attempt to describe to them that branch of science which specifically interests me. . . . The fact is I am a mystic, a transcendentalist, and a natural philosopher to boot. . . . How absurd that, though I probably stand as near to nature as any of them, and am by constitution as good an observer as most, yet a true account of my relation to nature should excite their ridicule only!"

He had no need for fear. No one is laughing at Thoreau's science today.

he wrote in *Walden*. "I desire that there may be as many different persons in the world as possible; but I would have each one be very careful to find out and pursue *his own* way, and not his father's or his mother's or his neighbor's instead." What folks can do is be inspired by his life and his words. And they can find their own paths as a result.

Here are a few examples of creative individuals who did just that.

Frank Lloyd Wright (1867–1959) was an American architect, designer, and writer. He endorsed the style of architecture called the Prairie School, believing that buildings should be constructed to work *with* nature, rather than *against* it. He had been influenced by Thoreau's writings, as well as those of Emerson and Walt Whitman. Wright read aloud passages from those books to his architectural students as they worked on their drawings at his Taliesin estate in Spring Green, Wisconsin.

J. E. H. MacDonald (1873–1932) was an English-born Canadian artist who most often painted views of nature. He was a founding member of Canada's Group of Seven, men who traveled around the country and painted colorful landscapes as seen through Canadian eyes. MacDonald and his wife Harriet admired Thoreau so much that they named their only child after him: Thoreau MacDonald. Thoreau would go on to become a renowned graphic artist himself.

N. C. Wyeth (1882–1945) was an American artist who created thousands of paintings and supplied illustrations for a number of books.

His mother-in-law introduced him to Thoreau's writings, and Wyeth became a fan. He drew 10 intricate color illustrations for the 1936 book, *Men of Concord and Some Others as Portrayed in the Journal of Henry David Thoreau*, edited by Francis H. Allen. Five of the 10 paintings are on permanent display in a reading room of the Concord Free Public Library.

E. B. White (1899–1985), author of the children's classic, *Charlotte's Web*, first read *Walden* when he was a student at Cornell University. It became the most influential book in his life. But when he visited Concord and Walden Pond in 1939, he wasn't impressed. He saw swimmers and boaters and litter lying around the park. He didn't think very highly of the cairn, even though he found a rock to add to it. "It is a rather ugly little heap of stones, Henry," he wrote. He walked back to the center of Concord along the railroad, as Thoreau had often done. Yet *Walden* still remained his favorite book.

Jane Langton (1922–   ) has written many books for children and adults, including the eight-part series called *The Hall Family Chronicles*. Langton first learned about Thoreau and the other transcendentalists in 1943, when she and her husband, Bill, moved to a house close to Walden Pond, in Lincoln, Massachusetts. She has taken Thoreau's words to heart, and she weaves his philosophies into her own books. In a 1994 interview printed in the *Concord Saunterer*, Langton said that in *The Fledgling* and the other Hall family books, "I'm saying the same thing over and over again, and that is, look, look, look. You don't need the magic. There is magic in this story, but you don't need magic. The magic is in the world. You want them to look and see and be aware, respond. That's all I say, because I think that's Thoreau."

D. B. Johnson (1944–   ) is the author and illustrator of *Henry Hikes to Fitchburg* and four other picture books bringing Thoreau to life as a bear. Johnson lives in New Hampshire, where he grew up and read *Walden* in high school. "I was surprised to hear the words of someone who loved the earth as much as I did," he says in a post on his website. "Later when I studied history and government in college, I read Thoreau's words again. This time I understood, not just his ideas about nature but also his philosophy about how to live. *If people weren't working so hard to buy stuff, he said, they could spend more time doing what they love.* That was an important idea. I decided to spend my life doing art."

Today admirers, students, and researchers can see Thoreau's original manuscripts in a number of large libraries and archives: the Special Collections department of the Concord Free Public Library in Concord, Massachusetts; the Thoreau Institute at Walden Woods in Lincoln, Massachusetts; the Morgan Library and Museum in New York City; the Henry W. and Albert A. Berg Collection at the New York Public Library in New York City; the Huntingdon Library in San Marino, California; and several others. The Concord Museum in Thoreau's hometown has his Walden house furniture and other belongings on display.

The homes of Thoreau's friends have been protected and opened to the public for many

Keep a Phenology

"I wanted to know my neighbors, if possible, —to get a little nearer to them. I soon found myself observing when plants first blossomed and leafed, and I followed it up early and late, far and near, several years in succession, running to different sides of the town and into the neighboring towns, often between twenty and thirty miles in a day. I often visited a particular plant four or five miles distant, half a dozen times within a fortnight, that I might know exactly when it opened, beside attending to a great many others in different directions and some of them equally distant, at the same time. At the same time I had an eye for birds and whatever else might offer."

Thoreau wrote this explanation in his journal on December 4, 1856. You don't have to be as meticulous or cover as much ground as he did. But just by watching the activity in your yard, neighborhood, park, or school grounds, you can create your own phenology. You can study nature's calendar and its recurring plant and animal life-cycle stages, such as birds migrating, flowers blooming, leaves emerging, etc. You can document the changes in the seasons and participate in "citizen science." If you keep these records for more than two years (or five, or ten, or more), you may even be able to track climate changes in your own region.

WHAT YOU NEED

- A notebook with pages lined in columns, or a computer spreadsheet file
- Pen or pencil
- Camera (optional)
- Keen powers of observation

Decide first where you will do your study. It should be a small property with some natural habitat, and one that you can easily access.

On the left-hand side of a lined piece of paper or on a computer spreadsheet, list the plants and animals that you know live here. Put one name in each box. Allow space below to add more later. If you don't know a proper name, give it a quick description for now, like "purple-leaf bush" or "brown striped bird."

You can start recording your observations at any time of year. The best time is in February or March, before spring officially begins. Go to your property every day, or every few days. Look for changes. Has a flower grown? Has a new bird arrived? Does the grass look greener than it did before? Is a bush sprouting berries? If your space is near a body of water, report on its appearance, too. Is the pond's water frozen? Is the stream muddy and flowing fast? Write the date and time of your first observations at the top of the first column on your spreadsheet. Then underneath, in the box next to the name of the plant or animal, write a brief note about what you saw. Use the next vertical column for the next day of your observations, and so on. You won't notice changes in every thing, every day. But over the course of the weeks and months, you'll see what happens as time passes.

This spreadsheet has room for only short notes. You can use your journal to write additional details of your experiences. You can take photographs of your finds, too.

You can check your observations with Henry's notes online at http://thoreauscalendar.umf.maine.edu. What has changed in a century and a half?

If you wish, you can even connect with other citizen scientists who live in other places. You can contribute your sightings to the general public knowledge about specific plants and animals. Networks where you can contribute your data include Cornell University's Project FeederWatch (www.birds.cornell.edu/pfw, with an annual participation fee), USA National Phenology Network (www.usanpn.org), and Bumble Bee Watch (www.bumblebeewatch.org). Ask an adult before you register to post your information online.

	March 3	April 6	
fox		Seems to be guarding a den, babies?	
brown striped bird	Building a nest		
maple tree	Small green buds	Full leaves, bright green	

years. Visitors can tour the houses of the Emersons, Alcotts, and Hawthornes. By contrast, the Thoreau family lived in nearly a dozen different houses during Henry's lifetime. Only one is open to the public: the house in which he was born. The building was moved farther along Virginia Road in 1878 and was lived in by others who were mostly farmers or farm workers. Concordians had known that Thoreau once lived here, and some would show it to out-of-towners. But it wasn't until after the last resident passed away in 1995 that the idea of saving Thoreau's birth house began to grow. The Thoreau Farm Trust was organized in 1998. In the early 2000s, funds were raised to purchase the property and to renovate

the house using best historical and environmental practices. It was named in the National Register of Historic Places in 2004. Thoreau Farm opened to the public in 2010.

Walden Pond recovered from its old amusement park stage. It was managed by Middlesex County and then by the Commonwealth of Massachusetts. But when the surrounding forest was threatened by two building projects in the late 1980s, local protesters were joined by national celebrities to form the Walden Woods Project to fight for preservation. They succeeded in dismissing the building plans. Today, Walden Pond State Reservation appeals to swimmers, fishermen, and hikers.

Visitors also come from around the world to pay tribute to someone they have read about and admire: Henry David Thoreau. He was a complex man. Yet his life was really only a beginning. His impact on us has deepened in the years that have passed. He has become a symbol for individual independence and environmentalism, and for taking a stand using civil disobedience. His words are firmly woven into the fabric of our culture, and his writings continue to touch people around the globe.

Thoreau paid close attention to what was going on around him, and he teaches us to do the same—no matter where we are, and no matter what time of year it is. "Live in each season as it passes," he wrote in his journal. "Breathe the air, drink the drink, taste the fruit, and resign yourself to the influences of each."

Skipping stones at Walden today.
Rob DePaolo

RESOURCES

WEBSITES TO EXPLORE

Huge amounts of information on Henry David Thoreau can be found on the Internet. The following sites are informative and reliable, and all have links to additional resources.

Botanical Index to the Journal of Henry David Thoreau
www.ray-a.com/ThoreauBotIdx
Compiled by Ray Angelo, longtime curator of the herbarium at Harvard University. This index will help you locate plant references in any journal entry. You will need a separate copy of the journal itself to follow the references.

The Concord Free Public Library's Special Collections
www.concordlibrary.org/scollect/thoreau.html
Owns nearly 200 property surveys conducted by Thoreau, as well as relevant letters and the manuscript of the essay "Walking." Many primary sources can be accessed online.

Concord Museum
www.concordmuseum.org
Features the Henry David Thoreau Collection, the largest grouping of items once owned by Thoreau or his family members. Browse the online catalog to see each piece, including the furniture from the Walden house.

Mapping Thoreau Country

www.mappingthoreaucountry.org

Uses historical maps to track many of Thoreau's travels and supplies links to a variety of primary source references that show his contributions to American philosophy and thought.

The Thoreau Institute at Walden Woods

www.walden.org/library

Provides the most comprehensive body of Thoreau-related material available in one place. Many resources are accessible online, including texts of all of Thoreau's books and essays, and a Mis-Quotation page that clears up questions of credit.

The Thoreau Reader

http://thoreau.eserver.org

Provides annotated online editions of Thoreau's writings, in addition to many more articles and essays about the man, his life, and his words.

The Thoreau Society

www.thoreausociety.org

Brings together scholars, fans, and appreciators of Thoreau, both online and in person at the Annual Gathering in Concord each July.

The Walden Woods Project

www.walden.org

Preserves the land, literature, and legacy surrounding Thoreau in order to foster environmental stewardship and social responsibility. Its offices and properties are within walking distance of Walden Pond.

The Writings of Henry David Thoreau

http://thoreau.library.ucsb.edu/

Known as the Princeton Editions Project, this academic office publishes the most complete volumes of Thoreau's writings by looking at his original handwritten manuscripts.

PLACES TO VISIT

Cape Cod National Seashore

99 Marconi Site Road

Wellfleet, Massachusetts 02667

www.nps.gov/caco/index.htm

This national park covers 40 miles of Atlantic Ocean shoreline. You can swim, walk, or bicycle here and follow in Thoreau's footsteps. You can visit lighthouses or consider what the pilgrims faced when they landed here nearly 400 years ago. Whales and dolphins often appear offshore too.

Monadnock State Park

116 Poole Road

Jaffrey, New Hampshire 03452

www.nhstateparks.org/explore/state-parks/monadnock-state-park.aspx

It's a rocky hike to the top of Monadnock, and the view is well worth the effort. Be sure to stop in the visitor center first to read what Thoreau wrote about the mountain. Campsites are available nearby.

Thoreau Farm: Birthplace of Henry David Thoreau

341 Virginia Road
Concord, Massachusetts 01742
www.thoreaufarm.org
Visit the house where Thoreau was born, and think about what started here. The house is open for weekend tours May through October, and throughout the year for special events.

Thoreau-Wabanaki Trail

c/o Maine Woods Forever
PO Box 692
Dover-Foxcroft, Maine 04426
thoreauwabanakitrail.org
Visit the web site first to see the map of Thoreau's travels through Maine, beginning in Bangor. You can join the route in Guilford, Greenville, or in another town as needed.

Wachusett Mountain State Reservation

345 Mountain Road
Princeton, Massachusetts 01541
www.mass.gov/eea/agencies/dcr/massparks/region-central/wachusett-mountain-state-reservation.html
See the same view of central Massachusetts that Thoreau did on the two occasions that he visited this favorite mountain. A visitor center and hiking trails are available throughout the year. Ski slopes are open in winter.

Walden Pond State Reservation

915 Walden Street
Concord, Massachusetts 01742
www.mass.gov/eea/agencies/dcr/massparks/region-north/walden-pond-state-reservation.html
Bring your hiking shoes and your bathing suit! A replica of Thoreau's house stands next to the parking lot. You can walk to the place where his house once stood.

NOTES

The entire collection of Thoreau's work can be found in the 20-volume set titled *The Writings of Henry David Thoreau*, published by Houghton Mifflin and Company in 1906. The entire text of this set is available online at www.walden.org/Library/The_Writings_of_Henry_David_Thoreau:_The_Digital_Collection.

The chart below explains which works are found in each volume of the full set. These volume numbers are cited in the following notes, along with the page numbers.

TITLE	SET VOLUME
A Week on the Condord . . .	1
Walden	2
Maine Woods	3
Cape Cod and Miscellanies	4
Excursions and Poems	5
Familiar Letters	6
Journal I	7
Journal II	8
Journal III	9
Journal IV	10

TITLE	SET VOLUME
Journal V	11
Journal VI	12
Journal VII	13
Journal VIII	14
Journal IX	15
Journal X	16
Journal XI	17
Journal XII	18
Journal XIII	19
Journal XIV	20

CHAPTER 1: AT HOME IN CONCORD

"I think I could write a poem to be called 'Concord' . . .": Thoreau, Entry dated September 4, 1841, in *Journal (I)*, vol. 7, 282.

"I have travelled a good deal in Concord . . .": Thoreau, "Economy," in *Walden*, vol. 2, 4.

"I have never gotten over my surprise . . .": Thoreau, Entry dated December 5, 1856, in *Journal (IX)*, vol. 15, 160.

"That woodland vision . . .": Thoreau, Entry dated August 1845, in *Journal (I)*, vol. 7, 381.

"sunshine and shadow . . .": Thoreau, Entry dated August 1845, in *Journal (I)*, vol. 7, 381.

"I would rather sit on a pumpkin . . .": Thoreau, "Economy," in *Walden*, vol. 2, 41.

"By the rude bridge . . .": Ralph Waldo Emerson, "Concord Hymn," in *The Portable Emerson*, Ed. by Carl Bode (New York: Penguin Books, 1981), 664.

"like-minded men and women . . .": Philip F. Gura, *American Transcendentalism: A History* (New York: Hill and Wang, 2007), 5.

"The happiest man is he who learns from nature . . .": Emerson, "Chapter VII: Spirit," in *Nature*, in *The Portable Emerson*, 41.

"In a journal it is important in a few words . . .": Thoreau, Entry dated February 5, 1855, in *Journal (VII)*, vol. 13, 171.

"painted green below, with a border of blue . . .": Thoreau, "Saturday," in *A Week on the Concord and Merrimack Rivers*, vol. 1, 12.

". . . I found myself again attending to plants . . .": Thoreau, Entry dated December 4, 1856, in *Journal (IX)*, vol. 15, 157.

standoffish, but was "not disagreeable . . .": Edward Waldo Emerson, *Henry Thoreau As Remembered by a Young Friend* (Mineola, NY: Dover Publications Inc., 1999 [reprint of 1917 original]), 9.

"I had lived three weeks beside it . . .": Nathaniel Hawthorne, "The Old Manse," in *Mosses from an Old Manse* (New York: The Modern Library, 2003), 5.

"acquire the aquatic skill of the owner . . .": Nathaniel Hawthorne, Entry for September 1, 1842, in *Passages from the American Notebooks*, vol. 2 (Boston: James R. Osgood and Company, 1876), 104.

"The fragrant white pond-lily abounds . . .": Hawthorne, "The Old Manse," 6.

"I spend a considerable portion . . .": Thoreau, entry dated March 23, 1856, in *Journal (VIII)*, vol. 14, 220.

"Grasshoppers have been very abundant . . .": Thoreau, Entry dated September 16, 1859, in *Journal (XII)*, vol. 18, 332.

"Why should I? I would not do again . . .": Emerson, "Thoreau," in *The Portable Emerson*, 573.

"The earth was uncommonly dry": Thoreau, Entry dated 1850, in *Journal (II)*, vol. 8, 22.

"The fire, we understand, was communicated to the woods . . .": *Concord Freeman*, May 3, 1844. As quoted in Walter Harding, *The Days of Henry Thoreau: A Biography* (New York, Dover Publications, Inc., 1982), 160–161.

Henry felt "like a guilty person . . .": Thoreau, Entry dated 1850, in *Journal (II)*, vol. 8, 23.

They called him a "damned rascal": Thoreau, Entry dated 1850, in *Journal (II)*, vol. 8, 25.

CHAPTER 2: WALDEN POND, *A WEEK*, AND *WALDEN*

"I see nothing for you in this earth . . .": William Ellery Channing, letter to Thoreau, March 5, 1845, in *The Writings of Henry D. Thoreau: The Correspondence, Volume I: 1834–1848*, Ed. by Robert N. Hudspeth (Princeton: Princeton University Press, 2013), 268.

"The scenery is romantic and pleasing . . .": *Boston Post*, June 13, 1844.

"I am refreshed and expanded . . .": Thoreau, "Sounds," in *Walden*, vol. 2, 132.

"I had three chairs in my house": Thoreau, "Visitors," in *Walden*, vol. 2, 155.

"I went to the woods because I wished . . .": Thoreau, "Where I Lived; and What I Lived For," in *Walden*, vol. 2, 100.

"It is worth the while to have lived . . .": Thoreau, Entry dated 1845–1846, in *Journal (I)*, vol. 7, 308.

"I have thus a tight shingled and plastered house . . .": Thoreau, "Economy," in *Walden*, vol. 2, 53.

"I think that I cannot preserve my health and spirits. . .": Thoreau, "Walking," in *Excursions and Poems*, vol. 5, 205.

"To be awake . . .": Thoreau, "Where I Lived; and What I Lived For," in *Walden*, vol. 2, 100.

"until I was aroused by the boat . . .": Thoreau, "The Ponds," in *Walden*, vol. 2, 213.

"I was determined to know beans . . .": Thoreau, "The Bean-Field," in *Walden*, vol. 2, 178.

"When they were growing . . .": Thoreau, "The Bean-Field," in *Walden*, vol. 2, 178.

"He who eats the fruit . . .": Thoreau, "Monday," in *A Week on the Concord and Merrimack Rivers*, vol. 1, 129.

"Making the earth say beans . . .": Thoreau, "The Bean-Field," in *Walden*, vol. 2, 173.

"Sometimes, in a summer morning . . .": Thoreau, "Sounds," in *Walden*, vol. 2, 123.

"How rarely a man's love for nature . . .": Thoreau, Entry dated April 23, 1857, in *Journal (IX)*, vol. 15, 337.

"It is remarkable how long men will believe . . .": Thoreau, "The Pond in Winter," in *Walden*, vol. 2, 315.

"What wonderful discoveries have been . . .": Thoreau, "Friday," in *A Week on the Concord and Merrimack Rivers*, vol. 1, 389.

"I have lately been surveying the Walden woods . . .": Thoreau, Entry dated January 1, 1858, in *Journal (X)*, vol. 16, 233.

"I left the woods for as good a reason . . .": Thoreau, "Conclusion," in *Walden*, vol. 2, 355.

"I learned this, at least, by my experiment . . .": Thoreau, "Conclusion," in *Walden*, vol. 2, 356.

"I have now a library of nearly nine hundred volumes . . .": Thoreau, Entry dated October 27, 1853, in *Journal (V)*, vol. 11, 459.

"Nevertheless, in spite of this result . . .": Thoreau, Entry dated October 27, 1853, in *Journal (V)*, vol. 11, 459.

"Our village life would stagnate . . .": Thoreau, "Spring," in *Walden*, vol. 2, 349–350.

"We need the tonic of wildness . . .": Thoreau, "Spring," in *Walden*, vol. 2, 350.

"We can never have enough of nature . . .": Thoreau, "Spring," in *Walden*, vol. 2, 350.

"I would not have any one adopt *my* mode . . .": Thoreau, "Economy," in *Walden*, vol. 2, 78.

"A lake is the landscape's most beautiful . . .": Thoreau, "The Ponds," in *Walden*, vol. 2, 206.

"Time is but the stream I go a-fishing in.": Thoreau, "Where I Lived; and What I Lived For," in *Walden*, vol. 2, 109.

"Heaven is under our feet . . .": Thoreau, "The Pond in Winter," in *Walden*, vol. 2, 313.

"The whistle of the locomotive . . .": Thoreau, "Sounds," in *Walden*, vol. 2, 128.

"On gala days the town fires its great guns . . ." Thoreau, "The Bean-Field," in *Walden*, vol. 2, 176.

"The finest qualities of our nature . . .": Thoreau, "Economy," in *Walden*, vol. 2, 7.

CHAPTER 3: CIVIL RIGHTS AND SOCIAL REFORMS

"The mass of men lead lives of quiet desperation": Thoreau, "Economy," in *Walden*, vol. 2, 8.

"To be awake is to be alive": Thoreau, "Where I Lived; and What I Lived For," in *Walden*, vol. 2, 100.

"As boys are sometimes required . . .": Thoreau, Entry dated January 3, 1861, in *Journal (XIV)*, vol. 20, 307.

"If a man does not keep pace with his companions . . .": Thoreau, "Conclusion," in *Walden*, vol. 2, 358

"You must have a genius [a talent] for charity . . .": Thoreau, "Economy," in *Walden*, vol. 2, 80.

"I'll pay your tax, Henry.": Edward Emerson, *Henry Thoreau as Remembered by a Young Friend* (Concord, MA: Thoreau Foundation, 1968), 64.

"It was like traveling into a far country . . .": Thoreau, "Civil Disobedience," in *Cape Cod and Miscellanies*, vol. 4, 378.

"I was released the next day, obtained my mended shoe . . .": Thoreau, "The Village," in *Walden*, vol. 2, 190.

"Henry, what are you doing in jail?": Jerome Lawrence and Robert E. Lee, *The Night Thoreau Spent in Jail: A Play* (New York: Hill and Wang, 1971; 2001 paperback edition), 67.

"I think that we should be men first . . .": Thoreau, "Civil Disobedience," in *Cape Cod and Miscellanies*, vol. 4, 358.

"I ask for, not at once no government . . .": Thoreau, "Civil Disobedience," in *Cape Cod and Miscellanies*, vol. 4, 357.

"Is a democracy, such as we know it . . .": Thoreau, "Civil Disobedience," in *Cape Cod and Miscellanies*, vol. 4, 387.

"There are thousands who are *in opinion* . . .": Thoreau, "Civil Disobedience," in *Cape Cod and Miscellanies*, vol. 4, 362.

"Even voting for the right is . . .": Thoreau, "Civil Disobedience," in *Cape Cod and Miscellanies*, vol. 4, 363.

Gandhi had read Thoreau's essays "with great pleasure . . .": James D. Hunt, *An American Looks at Gandhi: Essays in Satyagraha, Civil Rights and Peace* (New Delhi, India: Promilla & Co., 2005), 195.

"convincing and truthful": Hunt, *An American Looks at Gandhi*, 195.

"a great writer, philosopher, poet . . .": George Hendrick and Willene Hendrick, *Why Not Every Man? African Americans and Civil Disobedience in the Quest for the Dream* (Chicago: Ivan R. Dee, 2005), 144.

"Mahatma Gandhi never had more than one hundred persons . . .": Martin Luther King Jr., *Stride Toward Freedom: The Montgomery Story* (New York: Harper & Row, 1958), 218.

"I was so deeply moved that I reread . . .": Martin Luther King Jr., *The Autobiography of Martin Luther King, Jr.* Ed. by Clayborne Carson (New York: Warner Books, Inc., 1998), 14.

King found it "profound and electrifying.": King, *The Autobiography*, 23.

"At this point I began to think about Thoreau's *Essay* . . .": King, *The Autobiography*, 54.

"My mother was telling to-night of the sounds . . .": Thoreau, Entry dated May 26, 1857, in *Journal (IX)*, vol. 15, 381.

"5 p.m. Just put a fugitive . . .": Thoreau, Entry dated October 1, 1851, in *Journal (lll)*, vol. 9, 37.

"The effect of a good government . . .": Thoreau, "Slavery in Massachusetts," in *Cape Cod and Miscellanies*, vol. 4, 405.

"A government which deliberately . . .": Thoreau, "Slavery in Massachusetts," in *Cape Cod and Miscellanies*, vol. 4, 394.

"The fate of the country does not depend on how you vote . . .": Thoreau, "Slavery in Massachusetts," in *Cape Cod and Miscellanies*, vol. 4, 403.

He gave Brown "a trifling" amount: Thoreau, Entry dated October 22, 1859, in *Journal (Xll)*, vol. 18, 437.

"It galls me to listen to the remarks . . .": Thoreau, Entry dated October 18, 1859, in *Journal (XII)*, vol. 18, 401–402.

"He had the courage to face his country herself . . .": Thoreau, "A Plea for Captain John Brown," in *Cape Cod and Miscellanies*, vol. 4, 411.

"No man in America has ever . . .": Thoreau, "A Plea for Captain John Brown," in *Cape Cod and Miscellanies*, vol. 4, 425.

"I do not wish to kill nor to be killed . . .": Thoreau, "A Plea for Captain John Brown," in *Cape Cod and Miscellanies*, vol. 4, 433.

"I never hear of any particularly brave . . .": Thoreau, "The Last Days of John Brown," in *Cape Cod and Miscellanies*, vol. 4, 449.

"The greatest compliment that was ever paid me . . .": Thoreau, "Life Without Principle," in *Cape Cod and Miscellanies*, vol. 4, 455.

CHAPTER 4: EXPLORING NEW ENGLAND'S MOUNTAINS

"One must needs climb a hill . . .": Thoreau, Entry dated November 21, 1837, in *Journal (I)*, vol. 7, 12.

"Thus I admire the grandeur . . .": Thoreau, Entry dated November 21, 1837, in *Journal (I)*, vol. 7, 13.

"As we passed through the open country . . .": Thoreau, "A Walk to Wachusett," in *Excursions and Poems*, vol. 5, 136.

"We refreshed ourselves . . .": Thoreau, "A Walk to Wachusett," in *Excursions and Poems*, vol. 5, 140.

"The summit consists of a few acres . . .": Thoreau, "A Walk to Wachusett," in *Excursions and Poems*, vol. 5, 143.

"Wachusett is, in fact, the observatory . . .": Thoreau, "A Walk to Wachusett," in *Excursions and Poems*, vol. 5, 147.

"There lay Massachusetts . . ." Thoreau, "A Walk to Wachusett," in *Excursions and Poems*, vol. 5, 147.

"Monadnock, rearing its masculine front in the northwest . . .": Thoreau, "A Walk to Wachusett," in *Excursions and Poems*, vol. 5, 147–148.

"At length we saw the sun rise up out of the sea . . .": Thoreau, "A Walk to Wachusett," in *Excursions and Poems*, vol. 5, 146.

"But special I remember thee . . .": Thoreau, "A Walk to Wachusett," in *Excursions and Poems*, vol. 5, 135.

"With a glass you can see vessels in Boston Harbor . . .": Thoreau, Entry dated October 19, 1854, in *Journal (VII)*, vol. 13, 64.

"The universe is wider than our views of it.": Thoreau, "Conclusion," in *Walden*, vol. 2, 353.

"When you are on the mountain, the different peaks and ridges . . .": Thoreau, Entry dated June 4, 1858, in *Journal (X)*, vol. 16, 478.

"We lost the path coming down . . .": Thoreau, Entry dated June 2, 1858, in *Journal (X)*, vol. 16, 458.

"four hours from the time we were picking blueberries . . .": Thoreau, Entry dated September 7, 1852, in *Journal (IV)*, vol. 10, 347.

"One noon, when I was on the top . . .": Thoreau, Entry dated August 9, 1860, in *Journal (XIV)*, vol. 20, 36.

"They who simply climb to the peak . . .": Thoreau, Entry dated August 9, 1860, in *Journal (XIV)*, vol. 20, 39.

little clouds seemed bent on "forming and dissolving": Thoreau, Entry dated August 9, 1860, in *Journal (XIV)*, vol. 20, 47.

"I never saw a mountain that looked so high . . .": Thoreau, Entry dated August 6, 1860, in *Journal (XIV)*, vol. 20, 21.

"I carried on this excursion . . .": Thoreau, Entry dated August 9, 1860, in *Journal (XIV)*, vol. 20, 51–52.

"I had come over the hills on foot and alone . . .": Thoreau, "Tuesday," in *A Week on the Concord and Merrimack Rivers*, vol. 1, 189.

"Putting a little rice . . .": Thoreau, "Tuesday," in *A Week on the Concord and Merrimack Rivers*, vol. 1, 189.

"I reached the summit, just as the sun was setting. . . .": Thoreau, "Tuesday," in *A Week on the Concord and Merrimack Rivers*, vol. 1, 193.

"It would really be no small advantage . . .": Thoreau, "Tuesday," in *A Week on the Concord and Merrimack Rivers*, vol. 1, 197.

he was suddenly sailing on "an ocean of mist": Thoreau, "Tuesday," in *A Week on the Concord and Merrimack Rivers*, vol. 1, 197.

"There was not a crevice left through which the trivial places . . .": Thoreau, "Tuesday," in *A Week on the Concord and Merrimack Rivers*, vol. 1, 198.

There he "might hope to climb to heaven again": Thoreau, "Tuesday," in *A Week on the Concord and Merrimack Rivers*, vol. 1, 201.

"Two or three hours' walking will carry me . . .": Thoreau, "Walking," in *Excursions and Poems*, vol. 5, 211.

"The only roads were of Nature's making . . .": Thoreau, "Ktaadn," in *The Maine Woods*, vol. 3, 18.

"No face welcomed us . . .": Thoreau, "Ktaadn," in *The Maine Woods*, vol. 3, 39.

"and I mean to lay some emphasis . . .": Thoreau, "Ktaadn," in *The Maine Woods*, vol. 3, 66.

"The mountain seemed a vast aggregation . . .": Thoreau, "Ktaadn," in *The Maine Woods*, vol. 3, 69

"There it was, the State of Maine . . .": Thoreau, "Ktaadn," in *The Maine Woods*, vol. 3, 73.

"It is difficult to conceive of a region uninhabited by man. . . .": Thoreau, "Ktaadn," in *The Maine Woods*, vol. 3, 77.

"Think of our life in nature . . .": Thoreau, "Ktaadn," in *The Maine Woods*, vol. 3, 79.

"Going up there and being blown on is nothing. . . .": Thoreau, Letter to Harrison Gray Otis Blake, November 16, 1857, in *Letters to a Spiritual Seeker*, Ed. by Bradley P. Dean (New York: W. W. Norton & Company, 2004), 159.

"A man may use as simple a diet as the animals . . ." Thoreau, "Economy," in *Walden*, vol. 2, 68.

They were "lofty and bare . . .": Thoreau, Entry dated July 5, 1858, in *Journal (XI)*, vol. 17, 9.

"It is unwise for one to ramble over these mountains . . .": Thoreau, Entry dated July 8, 1858, in *Journal (XI)*, vol. 17, 22.

"A cloud may at any moment . . .": Thoreau, Entry dated July 8, 1858, in *Journal (XI)*, vol. 17, 22.

"If you take one side of a rock, and your companion another . . .": Thoreau, Entry dated July 19, 1858, in *Journal (XI)*, vol. 17, 58.

"I think that the top of Mt. Washington . . .": Thoreau, Entry dated January 3, 1861, in *Journal (XIV)*, vol. 20, 305

"I suppose that I feel the same awe . . .": Thoreau, Letter to Blake, in *Letters to a Spiritual Seeker*, 158.

CHAPTER 5: GOING FARTHER AFIELD

"I have travelled a good deal . . .": Thoreau, "Economy," in *Walden*, vol. 2, 4.

"Come & be Concord . . .": Thoreau, Letter to Blake, April 17, 1857, in *Letters to a Spiritual Seeker*, 149.

"It is a wild, rank place . . .": Thoreau, "IX: The Sea and The Desert," *Cape Cod*, in *Cape Cod and Miscellanies*, vol. 4, 186.

"Walking on the beach was out of the question . . .": Thoreau, "VII: Across the Cape," *Cape Cod*, in *Cape Cod and Miscellanies*, vol. 4, 146.

"If I had found one body cast upon the beach . . .": Thoreau, "II: The Shipwreck," *Cape Cod*, in *Cape Cod and Miscellanies*, vol. 4, 11.

"A man may stand there . . .": Thoreau, "X: Provincetown," *Cape Cod*, in *Cape Cod and Miscellanies*, vol. 4, 273.

"The time must come when this coast . . .": Thoreau, "X: Provincetown," *Cape Cod*, in *Cape Cod and Miscellanies*, vol. 4, 272–273.

"See a scum on the smooth surface of the lake . . .": Thoreau, Minnesota field notebook, 57. Held by Huntington Library (San Marino, California).

"We eagerly filled our pockets with the smooth round pebbles . . .": Thoreau, "VI: The Beach Again," *Cape Cod*, in *Cape Cod and Miscellanies*, vol. 4, 108.

"I wished only to be set down in Canada . . .": Thoreau, "I: Concord to Montreal," *A Yankee in Canada*, in *Excursions and Poems*, vol. 5, 3.

"It was a great cave in the midst of a city . . .": Thoreau, "I: Concord to Montreal," *A Yankee in Canada*, in *Excursions and Poems*, vol. 5, 13.

"Falls there are a drug . . .": Thoreau, "III: St. Anne," *A Yankee in Canada*, in *Excursions and Poems*, vol. 5, 58.

"We soon found that the inhabitants . . .": Thoreau, "II: Quebec and Montmorenci," *A Yankee in Canada*, in *Excursions and Poems*, vol. 5, 35.

"In Canada you are reminded of the government . . .": Thoreau, "IV: The Walls of Quebec," *A Yankee in Canada*, in *Excursions and Poems*, vol. 5, 83.

"You could see England's hands . . .": Thoreau, "I: Concord to Montreal," *A Yankee in Canada*, in *Excursions and Poems*, vol. 5, 16.

he might want to someday "make a longer excursion on foot . . .": Thoreau, "V: The Scenery of Quebec; and the River St. Lawrence," *A Yankee in Canada*, in *Excursions and Poems*, vol. 5, 101.

"What I got by going to Canada was a cold": Thoreau, "I: Concord to Montreal," *A Yankee in Canada*, in *Excursions and Poems*, vol. 5, 3.

"Found on reaching Fitchburg . . .": Thoreau, Entry dated September 5, 1856, in *Journal (IX)*, vol. 15, 61.

"Though I do not believe a plant will spring up . . .": Thoreau, "The Succession of Forest Trees," in *Excursions and Poems*, vol. 5, 203.

"A little mysterious hoeing and manuring . . .": Thoreau, "The Succession of Forest Trees," in *Excursions and Poems*, vol. 5, 203.

"Eastward I go only by force . . .": Thoreau, "Walking," in *Excursions and Poems*, vol. 5, 217.

"A regular council was held . . .": Thoreau, Letter to Frank Sanborn, June 25, 1861, in *The Correspondence of Henry David Thoreau*, Ed. by Walter Harding and Carl Bode (New York: New York University Press, 1958), 621.

"Here is a more interesting horizon . . .": Thoreau, Entry dated September 13, 1856, in *Journal (IX)*, vol. 15, 81.

CHAPTER 6: AN ENDURING LEGACY

"one of the most successful likenesses . . .": Daniel Ricketson, Letter to Sophia E. Thoreau, May 22, 1862, in *Daniel Ricketson and His Friends: Letters, Poems, Sketches, Etc.*, Ed. by Anna and Walton Ricketson (Boston: Houghton, Mifflin and Company, 1902), 146.

"I discover a slight shade . . .": Sophia E. Thoreau, Letter to Daniel Ricketson, May 26, 1862, in *Daniel Ricketson and His Friends*, 147.

"never saw a man dying with so much pleasure and peace": Walter Harding, *The Days of Henry Thoreau: A Biography* (New York: Dover Publications Inc., 1982), 460.

"I did not know we had ever quarreled": Edward Waldo Emerson, *Henry Thoreau As Remembered by a Young Friend* (Mineola, NY: Dover Publications Inc., 1999 [reprint of 1917 book]), 49.

"Now comes good sailing": Thomas Blanding, "A Last Word From Thoreau," *Concord Saunterer* 11.4 (Winter 1976): 16–17.

"No truer American existed than Thoreau . . .": Ralph Waldo Emerson, "Thoreau," in *The Portable Emerson*, Ed. by Carl Bode (New York: Penguin Books, 1981), 578.

"Every passage read by Mr. Blake . . .": Eliza Elvira Kenyon, "Excerpts from Ms. Eliza Elvira Kenyon's Journal," On file in the Archives Collections of the Plainfield Public Library (Plainfield, New Jersey).

"Mrs. Adams suggests that visitors to Walden shall bring . . .": Bronson Alcott, Entry dated June 12–13, 1872, *The Journals of Bronson Alcott* (Boston: Little, Brown and Company, 1938), 426.

"unsightly": James Dawson, "A History of the Cairn," *The Thoreau Society Bulletin* 232, Summer 2000, 3.

Whitman "stood a long while and ponder'd": Walt Whitman, *Specimen Days & Collect* (Philadelphia: David McKay, 1882), 190–191.

he rode "to Walden pond . . .": Whitman, *Specimen Days*, 191.

"I did not imagine I would be so moved . . .": William Frederic Bade, *The Life and Letters of John Muir* (Boston: Houghton Mifflin, 1924), vol. 2, 268.

"No wonder Thoreau lived here two years . . .": Bade, *The Life and Letters*, 268.

"rare sport tread in Emerson's tracks . . .": James Russell Lowell, *A Fable for Critics* (New York: Houghton, Mifflin & Co., 1890), 46.

"He only saw the things he looked for . . .": James Russell Lowell, "Thoreau," in *The Writings of James Russell Lowell*, vol. I, *Literary Essays* (Boston: Houghton, Mifflin and Company, 1890), 370.

"a mark of disease": Lowell, "Thoreau," 375.

"as perfect as anything in the language . . .": Lowell, "Thoreau," 380.

"In one word, Thoreau was a skulker": Robert Louis Stevenson, "Henry David Thoreau: His Character and Opinions (1880)," in Harold Bloom, *Bloom's Classic Critical Views: Henry David Thoreau* (New York: Bloom's Literary Criticism, 2008), 31.

"misdeeds": Stevenson, "Henry David Thoreau," 48.

"I will arise now and go . . .": William Butler Yeats, *Selected Poems* (New York: Gramercy Books, 1992), 57.

"to stimulate interest in and foster education about . . .": The Thoreau Society: About Us: Mission, Vision & Goals (website), www.thoreausociety.org/about, accessed August 3, 2015.

"Many a man has dated a new era . . .": Thoreau, "Reading," in *Walden*, vol. 2, 120.

"Heaven is under our feet as well as . . .": Thoreau, "The Pond in Winter," in *Walden*, vol. 2, 313.

"Simplicity, simplicity, simplicity! . . .": Thoreau, "Where I Lived; and What I Lived For," in *Walden*, vol. 2, 101.

"A man is rich in proportion to the number . . .": Thoreau, "Where I Lived; and What I Lived For," in *Walden*, vol. 2, 91.

"should not be able to attend . . .": Thoreau, Letter to Spencer F. Baird, December 19, 1853, in *The Correspondence of Henry David Thoreau*, Ed. by Walter Harding and Carl Bode (New York: New York University Press, 1958), 309.

"I felt that it would be to make myself the laughing-stock . . .": Thoreau, Entry dated March 5, 1853, in *Journal (V)*, vol. 11, 4.

"I wanted to know my neighbors, if possible . . .": Thoreau, Entry dated December 4, 1856, in *Journal (IX)*, vol. 15, 157.

"I would not have any one adopt *my* mode . . .": Thoreau, "Economy," in *Walden*, vol. 2, 78.

"It is a rather ugly little heap . . .": E. B. White, "Walden," *One Man's Meat* (New York: Harper & Row, 1944), 86.

"I'm saying the same thing": Roberta C. Martin, "An Interview with Jane Langton at Baker Farm, May 7th and 8th, 1994," *The Concord Saunterer*, New Series, Volume 2, Number 1, Fall 1994, 81.

"I was surprised to hear the words of someone . . .": D. B. Johnson, Quoted on "D. B. Johnson: About" (website), www.dbjohnsonart.com/about.html.

"Live in each season as it passes . . .": Thoreau, Entry dated August 23, 1853, in *Journal (V)*, vol. 11, 394.

BIBLIOGRAPHY

* *Books especially appropriate for young readers.*

*Burleigh, Robert, and Wendell Minor. *If You Spent a Day with Thoreau at Walden Pond*. New York: Henry Holt, 2012.

Chura, Patrick. *Thoreau the Land Surveyor*. Gainesville: University Press of Florida, 2010.

Emerson, Edward Waldo. *Henry Thoreau as Remembered by a Young Friend*. Mineola, NY: Dover, 1999.

Harding, Walter. *The Days of Henry Thoreau: A Biography*. 2nd edition. New York: Dover, 1982, 2011.

Huber, J. Parker. *The Wildest Country: Exploring Thoreau's Maine*. 2nd edition. Boston: Appalachian Mountain Club, 2008.

*Johnson, D. B. *Henry Hikes to Fitchburg*. Boston: Houghton Mifflin, 2000.

Maynard, W. Barksdale. *Walden Pond: A History*. New York: Oxford University Press, 2004.

*McCurdy, Michael. *Walden Then & Now: An Alphabetical Tour of Henry Thoreau's Pond*. Watertown, MA: Charlesbridge, 2010.

*Porcellino, John. *Thoreau at Walden*. New York: Hyperion, 2008.

*Reef, Catherine. *Henry David Thoreau: A Neighbor to Nature*. Frederick, MD: Twenty-first Century Books, 1992.

Richardson, Robert. *Henry Thoreau: A Life of the Mind*. Berkeley: University of California Press, 1988.

Sims, Michael. *The Adventures of Henry Thoreau: A Young Man's Unlikely Path to Walden Pond*. New York: Bloomsbury USA, 2014.

Smith, Harmon. *My Friend, My Friend: The Story of Thoreau's Relationship with Emerson*. Amherst: University of Massachusetts Press, 1999.

Stowell, Robert F. *A Thoreau Gazetteer*. Edited by William L. Howarth. Princeton, NJ: Princeton University Press, 1970.

Thoreau, Henry David. *The Quotable Thoreau*. Edited by Jeffrey S. Cramer. Princeton, NJ: Princeton University Press, 2011.

INDEX

THE ZIMMERMAN LIBRARY
SEVERN SCHOOL
201 WATER STREET
SEVERNA PARK, MD 21146